IN ASSOCIATION WITH

SQA

7

D1649733

HODDER GIBSON

Model Papers

WITH ANSWERS

PLUS: Official SQA 2014 & 2015 Past Papers With Answers

National 5
Modern Studies

Model Papers, 2014 & 2015 Exams

HODDER GIBSON
AN HACHETTE UK COMPANY

This book contains the official SQA 2014 and 2015 Exams for National 5 Modern Studies, with associated SQA approved answers modified from the official marking instructions that accompany the paper.

In addition the book contains model papers, together with answers, plus study skills advice. These papers, some of which may include a limited number of previously published SQA questions, have been specially commissioned by Hodder Gibson, and have been written by experienced senior teachers and examiners in line with the new National 5 syllabus and assessment outlines, Spring 2013. This is not SQA material but has been devised to provide further practice for National 5 examinations in 2014 and beyond.

Hodder Gibson is grateful to the copyright holders, as credited on the final page of the Answer Section, for permission to use their material. Every effort has been made to trace the copyright holders and to obtain their permission for the use of copyright material. Hodder Gibson will be happy to receive information allowing us to rectify any error or omission in future editions.

Hachette UK's policy is to use papers that are natural, renewable and recyclable products and made from wood grown in sustainable forests. The logging and manufacturing processes are expected to conform to the environmental regulations of the country of origin.

Orders: please contact Bookpoint Ltd, 130 Park Drive, Milton Park, Abingdon, Oxon OX14 4SE. Telephone: (44) 01235 827720. Fax: (44) 01235 400454. Lines are open 9.00–5.00, Monday to Saturday, with a 24-hour message answering service. Visit our website at www.hoddereducation.co.uk. Hodder Gibson can be contacted direct on: Tel: 0141 848 1609; Fax: 0141 889 6315; email: hoddergibson@hodder.co.uk

This collection first published in 2015 by
Hodder Gibson, an imprint of Hodder Education,
An Hachette UK Company
2a Christie Street
Paisley PA1 1NB

Typeset by Aptara, Inc.

Printed in the UK

A catalogue record for this title is available from the British Library

ISBN: 978-1-4718-6065-2

3 2 1

2016 2015

Introduction
Study Skills – what you need to know to pass exams!

Pause for thought

Many students might skip quickly through a page like this. After all, we all know how to revise. Do you really though?

Think about this:

"IF YOU ALWAYS DO WHAT YOU ALWAYS DO, YOU WILL ALWAYS GET WHAT YOU HAVE ALWAYS GOT."

Do you like the grades you get? Do you want to do better? If you get full marks in your assessment, then that's great! Change nothing! This section is just to help you get that little bit better than you already are.

There are two main parts to the advice on offer here. The first part highlights fairly obvious things but which are also very important. The second part makes suggestions about revision that you might not have thought about but which WILL help you.

Part 1

DOH! It's so obvious but …

Start revising in good time

Don't leave it until the last minute – this will make you panic.

Make a revision timetable that sets out work time AND play time.

Sleep and eat!

Obvious really, and very helpful. Avoid arguments or stressful things too – even games that wind you up. You need to be fit, awake and focused!

Know your place!

Make sure you know exactly **WHEN and WHERE** your exams are.

Know your enemy!

Make sure you know what to expect in the exam.

How is the paper structured?

How much time is there for each question?

What types of question are involved?

Which topics seem to come up time and time again?

Which topics are your strongest and which are your weakest?

Are all topics compulsory or are there choices?

Learn by DOING!

There is no substitute for past papers and practice papers – they are simply essential! Tackling this collection of papers and answers is exactly the right thing to be doing as your exams approach.

Part 2

People learn in different ways. Some like low light, some bright. Some like early morning, some like evening / night. Some prefer warm, some prefer cold. But everyone uses their BRAIN and the brain works when it is active. Passive learning – sitting gazing at notes – is the most INEFFICIENT way to learn anything. Below you will find tips and ideas for making your revision more effective and maybe even more enjoyable. What follows gets your brain active, and active learning works!

Activity 1 – Stop and review

Step 1

When you have done no more than 5 minutes of revision reading STOP!

Step 2

Write a heading in your own words which sums up the topic you have been revising.

Step 3

Write a summary of what you have revised in no more than two sentences. Don't fool yourself by saying, "I know it, but I cannot put it into words". That just means you don't know it well enough. If you cannot write your summary, revise that section again, knowing that you must write a summary at the end of it. Many of you will have notebooks full of blue/black ink writing. Many of the pages will not be especially attractive or memorable so try to liven them up a bit with colour as you are reviewing and rewriting. **This is a great memory aid, and memory is the most important thing.**

Activity 2 – Use technology!

Why should everything be written down? Have you thought about "mental" maps, diagrams, cartoons and colour to help you learn? And rather than write down notes, why not record your revision material?

What about having a text message revision session with friends? Keep in touch with them to find out how and what they are revising and share ideas and questions.

Why not make a video diary where you tell the camera what you are doing, what you think you have learned and what you still have to do? No one has to see or hear it, but the process of having to organise your thoughts in a formal way to explain something is a very important learning practice.

Be sure to make use of electronic files. You could begin to summarise your class notes. Your typing might be slow, but it will get faster and the typed notes will be easier to read than the scribbles in your class notes. Try to add different fonts and colours to make your work stand out. You can easily Google relevant pictures, cartoons and diagrams which you can copy and paste to make your work more attractive and **MEMORABLE**.

Activity 3 – This is it. Do this and you will know lots!

Step 1

In this task you must be very honest with yourself! Find the SQA syllabus for your subject (www.sqa.org.uk). Look at how it is broken down into main topics called MANDATORY knowledge. That means stuff you MUST know.

Step 2

BEFORE you do ANY revision on this topic, write a list of everything that you already know about the subject. It might be quite a long list but you only need to write it once. It shows you all the information that is already in your long-term memory so you know what parts you do not need to revise!

Step 3

Pick a chapter or section from your book or revision notes. Choose a fairly large section or a whole chapter to get the most out of this activity.

With a buddy, use Skype, Facetime, Twitter or any other communication you have, to play the game "If this is the answer, what is the question?". For example, if you are revising Geography and the answer you provide is "meander", your buddy would have to make up a question like "What is the word that describes a feature of a river where it flows slowly and bends often from side to side?".

Make up 10 "answers" based on the content of the chapter or section you are using. Give this to your buddy to solve while you solve theirs.

Step 4

Construct a wordsearch of at least 10 × 10 squares. You can make it as big as you like but keep it realistic. Work together with a group of friends. Many apps allow you to make wordsearch puzzles online. The words and phrases can go in any direction and phrases can be split. Your puzzle must only contain facts linked to the topic you are revising. Your task is to find 10 bits of information to hide in your puzzle, but you must not repeat information that you used in Step 3. DO NOT show where the words are. Fill up empty squares with random letters. Remember to keep a note of where your answers are hidden but do not show your friends. When you have a complete puzzle, exchange it with a friend to solve each other's puzzle.

Step 5

Now make up 10 questions (not "answers" this time) based on the same chapter used in the previous two tasks. Again, you must find NEW information that you have not yet used. Now it's getting hard to find that new information! Again, give your questions to a friend to answer.

Step 6

As you have been doing the puzzles, your brain has been actively searching for new information. Now write a NEW LIST that contains only the new information you have discovered when doing the puzzles. Your new list is the one to look at repeatedly for short bursts over the next few days. Try to remember more and more of it without looking at it. After a few days, you should be able to add words from your second list to your first list as you increase the information in your long-term memory.

FINALLY! Be inspired...

Make a list of different revision ideas and beside each one write **THINGS I HAVE** tried, **THINGS I WILL** try and **THINGS I MIGHT** try. Don't be scared of trying something new.

And remember – "FAIL TO PREPARE AND PREPARE TO FAIL!"

National 5 Modern Studies

The course

You will have studied the following three units:

- Democracy in Scotland and the United Kingdom
- Social Issues in the United Kingdom
- International Issues

Your teacher will usually have chosen one topic from each of the 3 sections above and you will answer questions on these in your exam (see table below).

SECTION 1	CHOICE ONE	CHOICE TWO
Democracy in Scotland and UK	A Democracy in Scotland	OR B Democracy in the UK
SECTION 2	CHOICE ONE	CHOICE TWO
Social Issues in the UK	C Social Inequality	OR D Crime and the Law
SECTION 3	CHOICE ONE	CHOICE TWO
International Issues	E World Powers	OR F World Issues

The Added Value unit for National 5 is an externally marked assessment. This consists of two parts:

- National 5 question paper
  60 marks allocated
  75% of marks
- National 5 assignment
  20 marks allocated
  25% of marks

Total marks available = 80

To gain the course award, all units and course assessments must be passed. The marks you achieve in the question paper and assignment are added together and an overall mark will indicate a pass or fail. From this, your course award will then be graded.

Question paper

You will have 1 hour and 30 minutes to complete the question paper, with a total of 60 marks allocated. There are 26 marks available for skills-based questions and 34 for knowledge and understanding, with 20 marks in total for each of the three exam sections as outlined in the table above.

In the exam paper, more marks are awarded for knowledge and understanding than skills so it is crucial that you have a sound grasp of content.

As stated, the paper will be divided into three sections, each worth 20 marks. Each section will have three questions. The three questions will be as follows:

Describe (worth either 4, 6 or 8 marks)
For example:
> Describe, in detail, at least two ways in which the police try to reduce crime levels.

Explain (worth either 4, 6 or 8 marks)
For example:
> Explain, in detail, why many people in the UK have good health while others do not.

Source-based (worth either out of 8 or 10)
For example:
> Using Sources 1, 2 and 3, what conclusions can be drawn about…?

What types of source-based questions will I need to answer?

There are three types of source-based skills questions and you will have practised these as class work. These three source-based skills questions are as follows:

- Using sources of information to identify and explain selective use of facts – this will have been assessed in your **Democracy in Scotland and UK unit**
- Using sources of information to make and justify a decision – this will have been assessed in your **Social Issues in the UK unit**
- Using sources of information to draw and support conclusions – this will have been assessed in your **International Issues unit.**

Remember, in your course exam the skills based questions can appear in any of the three units – so selective use of facts could be a question in the International Issues section of the exam.

Remember, in your course exam the knowledge and skills questions for International Issues will not refer to a particular country or issue. You will be expected to base your describe and explain answers around your knowledge and understanding of the World Power or World Issue you have studied.

What makes a good Knowledge and Understanding answer?

- Answer the question as set and only provide information relevant to the question.
- As far as you can, use up-to-date examples to illustrate your understanding of the question.

- Answer in detail and write in paragraphs with development of the points you wish to discuss. Remember, one very developed describe answer can gain 3 marks and one very developed explain answer can gain 4 marks.

- Show awareness of the difference between **describe** and **explain** questions and be able to answer appropriately.

- Use the number of marks given to each question as a guide to how much to write. Writing a long answer for a four mark question may cause you difficulty in completing the paper.

What makes a bad Knowledge and Understanding answer?

- Don't just write a list of facts. You will receive a maximum of two marks.

- Don't change the question to what you know – this is called *turning a question* and you will receive no marks for detailed description or explanation if it is not relevant.

- Avoid giving answers that are dated and too historical. This is especially a danger in the International Issues section.

- Don't rush together different issues, factors and explanations without developing your answer.

What makes a good Skills answer?

- Make full use of all the sources by linking evidence from more than one source to provide detailed arguments.

- Interpret statistical sources to indicate their significance to a question and how they link to other evidence.

- Make sure you use only the sources provided when writing your answers.

What makes a bad Skills answer?

- Don't use only a single piece of evidence from a source to provide argument.

- Don't simply repeat the statistical or written evidence without indicating its significance.

- Avoid bringing in your own knowledge of the issue or your own personal opinion.

Specific Skills advice

- For a selective use of facts answer, you should state whether the evidence being used is showing selectivity or not, and whether the evidence is supporting or opposing the view.

- For a conclusion answer, you should use the headings to draw an overall conclusion, which may be given at the beginning or end of the explanation.

- For a decision/recommendation answer, you should justify your decision and explain why you have rejected the other option.

Main Changes to Course Content

Democracy in Scotland and the United Kingdom

A study of the media is no longer optional and you must investigate the following:

- the impact of the media on election and democracy in Scotland or in the UK

- the case study choice is now either pressure groups or trade unions and their impact on elections and democracy in Scotland or in the UK

You will also examine the role of political parties in election campaigns in Scotland or in the UK in the election campaign section of the course.

International Issues

In the world issues section you should also study the possible motivations of international organisations in their attempts to resolve issues/conflicts. The international agencies explored are:

- The United Nations Organisation,

- Various NGOs,

- The European Union

- regional organisations (e.g. the African Union, NATO)

So you are now ready to answer the exam questions.

Good luck!

Remember that the rewards for passing National 5 Modern Studies are well worth it! Your pass will help you get the future you want for yourself. In the exam, be confident in your own ability. If you're not sure how to answer a question, trust your instincts and just give it a go anyway. Keep calm and don't panic! GOOD LUCK!

Model Paper 1

Whilst this Model Paper has been specially commissioned by Hodder Gibson for use as practice for the National 5 exams, the key reference documents remain the SQA Specimen Paper 2013 and the SQA Past Papers 2014 and 2015.

HODDER
GIBSON
LEARN MORE

National Qualifications MODEL PAPER 1

Modern Studies

Duration — 1 hour and 30 minutes

Total marks — 60

SECTION 1 — DEMOCRACY IN SCOTLAND AND THE UNITED KINGDOM — 20 marks

Attempt ONE part, EITHER

SECTION 2 — SOCIAL ISSUES IN THE UNITED KINGDOM — 20 marks

Attempt ONE part, EITHER

SECTION 3 — INTERNATIONAL ISSUES — 20 marks

Attempt ONE part, EITHER

Before attempting the questions you must check that your answer booklet is for the same subject and level as this question paper.

Read the questions carefully.

On the answer booklet, you must clearly identify the question number you are attempting.

Use **blue** or **black** ink.

Before leaving the examination room you must give your answer booklet to the Invigilator.
If you do not, you may lose all the marks for this paper.

MARKS

SECTION 1 — DEMOCRACY IN SCOTLAND AND THE UNITED KINGDOM — 20 marks

Attempt ONE part, either

Part A — Democracy in Scotland   on pages 2–4

OR

Part B — Democracy in the United Kingdom   on pages 5–7

PART A — DEMOCRACY IN SCOTLAND

In your answers to Questions 1 and 2 you should give recent examples from Scotland.

Question 1

> Decisions made about local services by councils can affect the lives of people in Scotland.

Describe, **in detail, two** ways in which decisions made about local services by councils can affect the lives of people in Scotland.   **4**

Question 2

> The Additional Member System (AMS) is used to elect the Scottish Parliament. Some people are happy with the way AMS has worked while others are unhappy.

Explain, **in detail**, why some people are happy with the way the Additional Member System (AMS) of voting has worked while others are unhappy.   **8**

Part A (continued)

Question 3

Study Sources 1, 2 and 3 below, then attempt the question which follows.

SOURCE 1

New Tax Powers Proposed for Scottish Parliament

More than 10 years after devolution was introduced in Scotland, there have been calls for more powers to be given to the Scottish Parliament. Greater tax-raising powers have been proposed for the Parliament. The new proposal would work by cutting the amount of money from the block grant, which the Scottish Government receives from the UK Government and reducing the rate of income tax in Scotland by 10p. MSPs would then have to decide what to do:

- either set the "Scottish tax rate" at 10p so the amount of cash Scotland will get would stay the same

- or cut the rate to less than 10p and people's taxes would fall, but there would be a reduction in public spending

- or set a tax rate higher than 10p and be able to spend more on public services.

Some have argued against this change as it could lead to higher taxes in Scotland compared to England. It may also, as stated, give the UK government an excuse to reduce the funding to the Scottish Government and Parliament. This financial reduction could lead to a crisis in our hospitals and schools, given the significant cuts already made to the public sector. It could lead to a decrease in the Scottish public's trust of the Scottish Government

Supporters of the proposal see it as the next step to increase the powers of the devolved Parliament, now that it is well established and trusted by the Scottish people. It would also make the Parliament more accountable, as voters would be able to choose the party which had the tax and spending policies they support. There would be fewer arguments between the UK Government and the Scottish Government about money as the Scottish Government would have greater control over its own spending decisions.

SOURCE 2

Public Opinion Survey: Who has the most influence over the way Scotland is run?						
	1999	2001	2003	2005	2007	2009
Scottish Government/ Scottish Parliament	13%	15%	17%	23%	28%	33%
United Kingdom Government/United Kingdom Parliament	66%	66%	64%	47%	47%	39%

Part A Question 3 (continued)

SOURCE 3

Percentage of People who Trust the UK and Scottish Governments to Act in Scotland's Interests

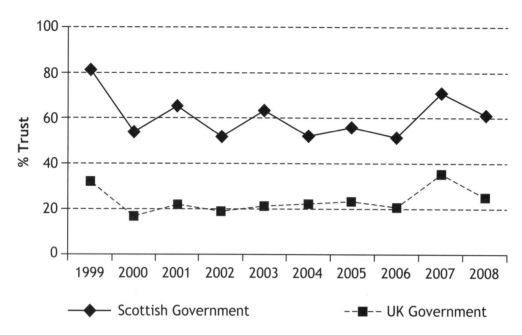

Using Sources 1, 2 and 3 above, explain why the view of Gillian Duffy is **selective in the use of facts.**

> **New tax-raising powers for the Scottish Parliament would be good for Scotland.**
>
> **View of Gillian Duffy**

In your answer you must:

give evidence from the sources that supports Gillian Duffy's view

and

give evidence from the sources that opposes Gillian Duffy's view.

Your answer must be based on all three sources.

8

NOW GO TO SECTION 2 ON *PAGE EIGHT*

PART B — DEMOCRACY IN THE UNITED KINGDOM

In your answers to Questions 1 and 2 you should give recent examples from the United Kingdom.

Question 1

> The House of Lords plays a part in decision making in the UK.

Describe, **in detail**, **two** ways in which the House of Lords plays a part in decision making in the UK.

4

Question 2

Media	Trade Unions	Pressure Groups

Choose **one** of the above.

Explain, **in detail**, why some people think they play a positive role in politics while others believe they play a negative role in politics.

8

Part B (continued)

MARKS

Question 3

Study Sources 1, 2 and 3 below, then attempt the question which follows.

SOURCE 1

Party Leaders' Debates Change Election Campaign

When the General Election was called for in April 2010, many people thought that the campaign would be of little interest. The Conservative Party had been far ahead of Labour in the opinion polls for many months. It was predicted that David Cameron and the Conservative Party would win the election. For the first time in the UK, televised leaders' debates were held. The three main political parties agreed to hold three debates involving Gordon Brown (Labour), David Cameron (Conservative) and Nick Clegg (Liberal Democrats). The first debate had a major impact on the opinion polls; Nick Clegg was thought to have done well. His strong performance, compared to the other leaders, saw the Liberal Democrats rise in the opinion polls and turned a "two-horse race" between Labour and the Conservatives into a real contest between the three parties.

Many people felt the debates focused too much on the personality of the leaders at the expense of local campaigns; and image and style were seen to be more important than policies. Some people believed the debates would have little impact on the result as most people had made up their minds, before the election, about who they would vote for. Millions of viewers watched the debates and turnout increased in the 2010 election to 65·1%, up 4% on 2005. Labour lost the election; Gordon Brown was thought to have done poorly in the debates. After the votes were counted, no party had an overall majority so a coalition government was formed by the Conservative Party, which was the largest party, and the Liberal Democrats. David Cameron became Prime Minister with Nick Clegg as his deputy.

SOURCE 2

Do you think the leaders' debates were a positive or negative change to the election campaign?

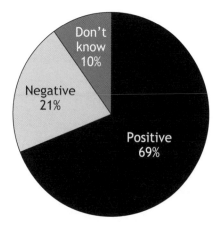

Did the leaders' debates make a difference to how you cast your vote at the general election?

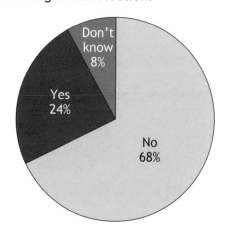

Part B Question 3 (continued)

SOURCE 3

Who do you think performed best overall in the party leaders' debates?			
	1st debate	**2nd debate**	**3rd debate**
Gordon Brown (Labour)	19%	29%	25%
David Cameron (Conservative)	29%	36%	41%
Nick Clegg (Liberal Democrats)	51%	32%	32%
Number of viewers (Channel debate shown on)	9·4m (ITV)	4·1m (Sky)	8·4m (BBC)

All figures from YouGov

Using Sources 1, 2 and 3 above, explain why the view of Adam Stewart is **selective in the use of facts.**

> **The party leaders' debates in the 2010 election had little impact on the election campaign.**
>
> **View of Adam Stewart**

In your answer you must:

give evidence from the sources that supports Adam Stewart's view

and

give evidence from the sources that opposes Adam Stewart's view.

Your answer must be based on all three sources.   8

NOW GO TO SECTION 2 ON *PAGE EIGHT*

MARKS | DO NOT WRITE IN THIS MARGIN

SECTION 2 — SOCIAL ISSUES THE UNITED KINGDOM — 20 marks

Attempt ONE part, either

Part C — Social Inequality   on pages 8–11

OR

Part D — Crime and the Law   on pages 12–14

PART C — SOCIAL INEQUALITY

In your answers to Questions 1 and 2 you should give recent examples from Scotland.

Question 1

Government has tried to improve the health of people in Scotland.

Describe, **in detail**, **two** ways in which the Government has tried to improve the health of people in Scotland.   **4**

Question 2

Some people live in poverty in the United Kingdom.

Explain, **in detail**, why some people live in poverty in the United Kingdom.   **6**

Part C (continued)   MARKS

Question 3

Study Sources 1, 2 and 3 below, then attempt the question which follows.

You are an adviser to the UK Government. You have been asked to recommend whether or not the Government should continue with the system of Working Tax Credits (WTC) as part of Universal Credit or not to continue with the system.

| **Option 1**
Continue with the system of
Working Tax Credits. | **Option 2**
Do not continue with the system
of Working Tax Credits. |

SOURCE 1

Facts and Viewpoints

Working Tax Credit (WTC), introduced in 2003, can be given to top up earnings if a person is in work but on low pay. You can get WTC if you are over 16 years old and work more than 16 hours per week and are also either a parent or responsible for children.

- Working Tax Credits help people to beat the poverty trap — it makes sure a person's income is better in work than out of work and living on benefits.

- There have been problems in the system with overpayments being made and then having to be paid back.

- The basic amount awarded is £1,730 per year, with extra payments depending on circumstances.

- Many families have suffered hardship when attempts have been made to recover overpayments made to them, which many poor families have already spent.

- In 2005, the Working Tax Credit website was closed down because of a high level of fraudulent claims by organised criminals.

- Working Tax Credits have been criticised as they encourage employers to pay low wages.

- Over half a million children have been lifted out of poverty as more people on low or moderate incomes have been helped; more than through any other single measure.

- Over half the overpayment errors made affected those in the lowest income group — the very people who will struggle to pay them back.

- Working Tax Credit allows families to get back up to 80% of the cost of childcare allowing adults to go back to work; this can be as much as £175 per week for one child and up to £300 per week for two or more children.

Part C Question 3 (continued)

SOURCE 2

Error and Fraud in Working Tax Credit System (2004–2005)

	Number of Cases of Error and Fraud	Amount Involved in Error and Fraud
2005	1,460,000	£2,440 million
2010	1,400,000	£2,660 million

Number of Children in Poverty: 2001–2010

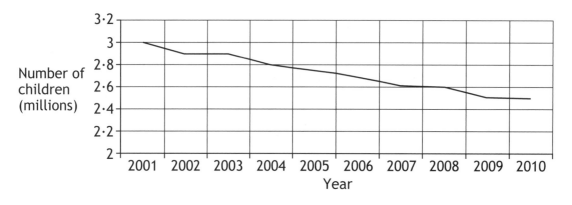

Part C Question 3 (continued)

SOURCE 3

Viewpoints

The Government should not continue with the system of Working Tax Credits. To date, the personal details of over 10,000 public sector workers had been stolen by organised tax criminals to be used to claim tax credits. Fraud and mistakes led to huge losses. People have to notify the tax authorities when their pay rises. If they do not do this then they have to pay the overpaid WTC back. The stress that this has caused families can have a damaging effect on the children. Working Tax Credit should be scrapped and replaced by a simpler system.

Pressure Group Spokesperson

The Government should continue with the system of Working Tax Credits. In the past, when people went from benefits to work, they lost some means-tested benefits. The problem faced by many was that if they came off benefits and went into low paid jobs, they were worse off. There was little to motivate people to find work. Working Tax Credits encourage people to work and also give help with childcare costs. Despite problems with overpayments in the first few years, many of these difficulties have now been sorted. The tax credit system has helped many families to get out of poverty.

Government Spokesperson

You must decide which option to recommend to the Government, **either** to continue with the system of Working Tax Credits (**Option 1**) or not to continue with the system of Working Tax Credits (**Option 2**).

(i) Using Sources 1, 2 and 3 above and opposite, **which option would you choose**?

(ii) Give reasons to **support** your choice.

(iii) **Explain** why you did not choose the other option.

Your answer must be based on all three sources.

10

NOW GO TO SECTION 3 ON *PAGE FIFTEEN*

PART D — CRIME AND THE LAW

In your answers to Questions 1 and 2 you should give recent examples from the United Kingdom.

Question 1

> Some young people commit crimes.

Describe, **in detail**, **two** crimes most commonly committed by young people.   **4**

Question 2

> In some areas community policing is the best way to tackle crime, while in others the use of CCTV cameras is better.

Explain, **in detail**, why in some areas community policing is the best way to tackle crime, while in others the use of CCTV cameras is better.   **6**

Part D (continued)

Question 3

Study Sources 1, 2 and 3 below, then attempt the question which follows.

You are an adviser to the Scottish Government. You have been asked to recommend whether the DNA database should contain profiles of the whole population or keep the DNA database for profiles of convicted criminals only.

| **Option 1** The DNA database should contain profiles of the whole population. | **Option 2** The DNA database should contain profiles of convicted criminals only. |

SOURCE 1

Facts and Viewpoints

In Scotland, only convicted criminals have their DNA profile stored on the DNA database. The profile contains details about individuals, which can be used for investigating crimes.

- If the whole adult population had their DNA profiles on the database, this would help in the investigation and prosecution of crime.

- To expand the database to include the whole population would be very expensive.

- Most people would approve of a new law requiring all adults to give a sample of their DNA to help with prevention and detection of crime.

- Money and time would be saved if everyone's DNA profile was taken only once.

- If a person's DNA is found to be present at a crime scene they could be viewed as guilty without any other supporting evidence.

- Currently, there are not enough safeguards in place to ensure that there is no misuse of DNA information.

- DNA evidence is not foolproof and may lead to wrongful convictions.

- Ethnic minorities are more likely, at present, to be on the database than white people.

- DNA databases are only as reliable as those who handle them — there are many spelling errors and inaccuracies in the storage of information.

SOURCE 2

Ethnic Group	% of Ethnic Group on Database
White	9
Asian	13
Black	37

Part D Question 3 (continued)   MARKS   DO NOT WRITE IN THIS MARGIN

Result of Opinion Poll Survey

Should there be a new law requiring everyone over 18 to give a sample of DNA?	
Yes – 66%	No – 33%

If you were to serve on a jury would you count DNA evidence as more or less important than other evidence?		
More important – 65%	Less important – 4%	Equally important – 28%

SOURCE 3

Viewpoints

The DNA database should contain profiles of the whole population. The current system is unfair. It would be fairer to include everybody, guilty or innocent. Having everyone on the database means there will be no discrimination against ethnic minorities. Civil liberties groups and representatives of the black community say that the existing database reinforces racial bias in the criminal justice system. DNA evidence will not be used in all cases, but will help the police convict the right person in the most serious of crimes.

Police Spokesperson

The DNA database should be kept for profiles of convicted criminals only. The Universal Declaration of Human Rights states that everyone has the right to protection of their privacy in their family or home life. To have everyone's DNA profile on the database would mean innocent people are having their rights abused. If two people meet on the street and shake hands their DNA is transferred. If one of these people then commits a crime, the DNA of the person he or she shook hands with could be found at the crime scene. DNA evidence is not the answer to solving the great majority of crimes.

Civil Rights Spokesperson

You must decide which option to recommend to the Scottish Government, **either** the DNA database should contain profiles of the whole population (**Option 1**) **or** the DNA database should contain profiles of convicted criminals only (**Option 2**).

(i)   Using Sources 1, 2 and 3 above, **which option would you choose?**

(ii) Give reasons to **support** your choice.

(iii) **Explain** why you did not make the other choice.

Your answer must be based on all three sources.   10

NOW GO TO SECTION 3 ON *PAGE FIFTEEN*

MARKS DO NOT WRITE IN THIS MARGIN

SECTION 3 — INTERNATIONAL ISSUES — 20 marks

Attempt ONE part, either

Part E — World Powers **on pages 15–17**

OR

Part F — World Issues **on pages 18–20**

PART E — WORLD POWERS

In your answers to Questions 1 and 2 you should give recent examples from a world power you have studied.

Question 1

All governments have different political institutions.

Describe, **in detail**, at least two main political institutions of the government of a world power you have studied. 6

Question 2

Social problems faced by world powers			
Poor education	Health inequalities	Fear of crime	Poor housing

Choose **one** of the social problems shown above.

Explain, **in detail,** why this issue continues to be a problem in a world power you have studied. 6

Part E (continued)

Question 3

Study Sources 1, 2 and 3 below, then attempt the question which follows.

SOURCE 1

Life in the G20 Country

This G20 state is a very large country with the world's biggest population of around 1.3 billion people. It is made up of a variety of different regions and ethnic groups. The largest ethnic group, by far, is the Han whose language remains the most common language throughout most of the country. Population and language spoken varies across the nation. There are 29 provinces and the part of the country where a person lives can have a major effect upon his or her life.

The average income is rising as the country becomes more prosperous. However, there are big differences in levels of income between different parts of the country, especially between rural and urban areas. Income differences are important because they have an effect upon success in education.

There are large differences in health and education between rural and urban areas. Urban areas tend to have better schools and health care. Since most of the wealthy people live in the cities they are able to afford the best in education and health. Rural areas are poorer and so too are education and health facilities.

Overall, the country is making very good progress and many people are becoming wealthy and enjoy a good standard of living. However, people in some parts enjoy a better life than people in other areas. Areas on the coast have benefited more from foreign investment. Coastal areas have more industry and tend to be better off with more manufacturing and service jobs and growing wealth.

SOURCE 2

Social and Economic Information about Life in Selected Regions

	Shanghai	Beijing	Beijing Guangdong	Yunnan	Guizhou	Tibet
Population	17.8 million	15.4 million	91.9 million	44.4 million	37.3 million	2.8 million
% Urban	89.0%	83.6%	60.7%	29.5%	26.9%	26.8%
% Rural	11.0%	16.4%	39.3%	70.5%	73.1%	73.4%
Life Expectancy (in years)	78	76	73	65	66	64
Percentage unable to read or write	5.9%	4.6%	7.6%	21.5%	19.7%	54.9%
Average Income per person (in Yuan)	46 718	32 061	17 213	5662	3603	6871

Part E Question 3 (continued)

SOURCE 3

Information about Ethnic Composition in Selected Regions

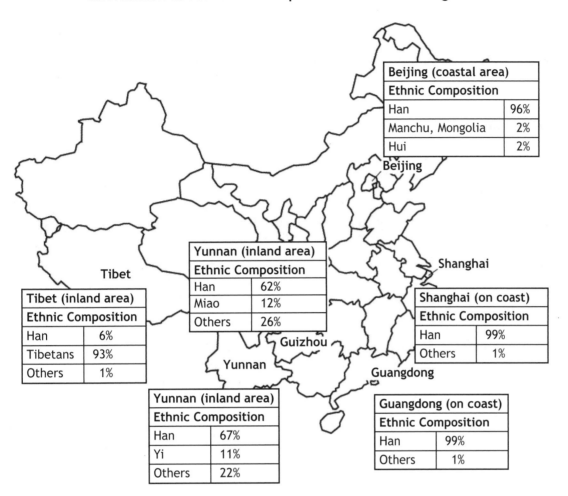

Beijing (coastal area)	
Ethnic Composition	
Han	96%
Manchu, Mongolia	2%
Hui	2%

Yunnan (inland area)	
Ethnic Composition	
Han	62%
Miao	12%
Others	26%

Tibet (inland area)	
Ethnic Composition	
Han	6%
Tibetans	93%
Others	1%

Shanghai (on coast)	
Ethnic Composition	
Han	99%
Others	1%

Yunnan (inland area)	
Ethnic Composition	
Han	67%
Yi	11%
Others	22%

Guangdong (on coast)	
Ethnic Composition	
Han	99%
Others	1%

Using Sources 1, 2 and 3 above, what **conclusions** can be drawn about life in the selected country?

You should reach a conclusion about each of the following:

- ethnic composition in different parts of the country

- the link between income and education

- health in urban and rural areas.

Your conclusions must be supported by evidence from the sources. You should link information within and between sources in support of your conclusions.

Your answer must be based on all three sources.

8

PART F — WORLD ISSUES

In your answers to Questions 1 and 2 you should give recent examples from a world issue you have studied.

Question 1

> There are often a variety of factors which cause an international issue or problem.

Describe, **in detail**, at least two causes of an international issue or problem you have studied.

6

Question 2

International organisations which try to resolve international issues and problems		
NATO	European Union	African Union
United Nations Organisation	Charities and other NGOs	World Bank

Explain, **in detail**, why international organisations experience problems in trying to resolve an international issue you have studied.

6

Part F (continued)

Question 3

Study Sources 1, 2, 3 and 4 below, then attempt the question which follows.

SOURCE 1

The G8 Promise to Africa

The G8 countries are Canada, France, Germany, Italy, Japan, Russia, the United Kingdom and the United States. They are the world's major industrialised democracies. On many occasions these G8 countries have committed themselves to giving the UN recommendation of 0·7% of Gross National Income (GNI) as Official Development Assistance (ODA). It is felt that this would help achieve dramatic progress in the fight against poverty in Africa. At the 2005 "Make Poverty History" G8 summit at Gleneagles, Scotland, they promised to do the following by the 2010 G8 summit in Canada:

Promise 1: To improve health care

Promise 2: To more than double total ODA given to all less developed countries by 2010

Promise 3: To improve education

Promise 4: To deliver a $22·6 billion increase in ODA to sub-Saharan Africa between 2005 and 2010.

In terms of total ODA to all less developed countries, the G8 countries have all increased their contribution, with Canada almost doubling its ODA contribution. Recent health and education figures have been encouraging. Between 1996 and 2009 the % of HIV sufferers in Rwanda has declined from 7.0 % to 2.8%.

SOURCE 2

Total ODA given by selected G8 countries to all less developed countries

Selected G8 Countries	2005		2007		2010	
	ODA $ Billions	% of GNI	ODA $ Billions	% of GNI	ODA $ Billions	% of GNI
Canada	2·6	0·27	4·1	0·29	5·1	0·33
France	8·5	0·41	9·9	0·38	12·9	0·50
Germany	7·5	0·28	12·3	0·37	12·7	0·38
Italy	2·5	0·15	4·0	0·19	3·1	0·15
Japan	8·9	0·19	7·7	0·17	11·0	0·20
United Kingdom	7·9	0·36	9·9	0·35	13·8	0·56
USA	19·7	0·17	21·8	0·19	30·0	0·21

Part F Question 3 (continued)

SOURCE 3

Health and Education Statistics

	Burundi		Ethiopia		Malawi	
	1996	2009	1996	2009	1996	2009
HIV % (age 15-49)	5·2	2·0	2·4	2·1	12·1	11·9
Infant Mortality Rate per 1000 Births	112	102	108	69	122	65
Life Expectancy at Birth (years)	45	51	49	56	52	53
% Primary School Completion	25	45	14	46	48	55
% Literacy Rate—females 15-24	48	75	28	40	65	85
% Literacy Rate—males 15-24	59	77	39	65	75	87

Using only the information in Sources 1, 2 and 3 above, what **conclusions** can be made about the G8 and aid to African countries?

You should reach a conclusion about each of the following:

- the success of the G8 in meeting Promise 1

- the success of the G8 in meeting Promise 2

- the G8 country most committed to meet the UN aid recommendation.

8

Your conclusions must be supported by evidence from the sources. You should link information within and between the sources in support of your conclusions.

Your answer must be based on all three sources.

[END OF MODEL PAPER 1]

Model Paper 2

Whilst this Model Paper has been specially commissioned by Hodder Gibson for use as practice for the National 5 exams, the key reference documents remain the SQA Specimen Paper 2013 and the SQA Past Papers 2014 and 2015.

NATIONAL 5 MODERN STUDIES 30 HODDER GIBSON MODEL PAPER 2

N5

National
Qualifications
MODEL PAPER 2

Modern Studies

Duration — 1 hour and 30 minutes

Total marks — 60

SECTION 1 — DEMOCRACY IN SCOTLAND AND THE UNITED KINGDOM — 20 marks

Attempt ONE part, EITHER

SECTION 2 — SOCIAL ISSUES IN THE UNITED KINGDOM — 20 marks

Attempt ONE part, EITHER

SECTION 3 — INTERNATIONAL ISSUES — 20 marks

Attempt ONE part, EITHER

Before attempting the questions you must check that your answer booklet is for the same subject and level as this question paper.

Read the questions carefully.

On the answer booklet, you must clearly identify the question number you are attempting.

Use **blue** or **black** ink.

Before leaving the examination room you must give your answer booklet to the Invigilator. If you do not, you may lose all the marks for this paper.

HODDER GIBSON
LEARN MORE

MARKS

SECTION 1 — DEMOCRACY IN SCOTLAND AND THE UNITED KINGDOM — 20 marks

Attempt ONE part, either

Part A — Democracy in Scotland   on pages 2–5

OR

Part B — Democracy in the United Kingdom   on pages 6–8

PART A — DEMOCRACY IN SCOTLAND

In your answers to Questions 1 and 2 you should give recent examples from Scotland.

Question 1

The Scottish Parliament can make decisions about devolved matters for Scotland.

Describe, **in detail**, **two** devolved matters which the Scottish Parliament can make decisions about for Scotland.

4

Question 2

Local councils in Scotland can raise money in different ways.

Explain, **in detail**, at least two ways in which local councils in Scotland can raise money.

6

NOW ATTEMPT QUESTION 3

Part A (continued)   MARKS

Question 3

Study Sources 1, 2 and 3 below, then attempt the question which follows.

You have been asked to recommend who should be your party's candidate in the local council elections.

Option 1	Option 2
Candidate Ian McKay	Candidate Sally Anderson

SOURCE 1

Selected Facts About Inverdon

Inverdon is a council area in the north east of Scotland. It has a population of 263,000 which has significantly grown in recent years due to an inflow of migrant workers mainly from Eastern Europe. They have been useful to local business as they often find work on farms and in other low-paid jobs. Unemployment amongst this group of migrant workers is very low.

Like all Scottish local authorities, Inverdon Council has been facing great financial difficulties in recent years. This has been due to less money coming from the Scottish Government to it and a decision to freeze the level of council tax paid by residents.

Selected Economic Statistics			
	Inverdon	Glasgow	Scotland
Average Weekly Pay	£450	£475	£455
Unemployment	4·2%	5·9%	4·0%

Selected Housing Statistics about Inverdon			
	2009	2010	2011
Average House Price (£000s)	210	185	200
Houses Built	2105	1226	950

Part A Question 3 (continued)

MARKS

SOURCE 2

Inverdon Dunes Golf Development	
Golf Development Company	**Save Our Dunes Campaign**
A large American company is seeking planning permission for a massive £750 million development. It will consist of two golf courses, a large 400-bed hotel and leisure complex, and 200 holiday homes for short-term rental.	A local pressure group has been set up to oppose the golf development. They have a number of concerns.
There will also be accommodation for 400 staff. A separate housing development nearby will make 300 homes available for sale, with prices starting at £600,000 per house.	They believe that the 4000-year-old dune system will be destroyed whilst 6 holes of the new golf course will be built on a Site of Special Scientific Interest, which is protected by current law.
It is expected that the development will be a big boost to the local economy, as it will provide 5000 temporary construction jobs and 1250 permanent jobs. It is estimated that it will attract over 100,000 "golf tourists" from all over the world each year.	They are also of the opinion that roads will become busier leading to more congestion and air pollution.
	It is estimated that about 25,000 tourists already visit the area annually to enjoy the unspoilt views, the rare plants and animal species on the dunes. They believe that these visitors will no longer come.

SOURCE 3

Survey of Public Opinion in Inverdon			
	Yes	No	Don't Know
Do you support the Inverdon Dunes Golf Development?	65%	25%	10%
Do you think that Inverdon Council is doing a good job?	35%	43%	22%
Do you think that Inverdon needs more migrant workers?	32%	55%	13%

Part A Question 3 (continued)

MARKS

Information about the Two Candidates

Ian McKay

- I support the golf development. If elected, I will always welcome employment opportunities, and this development will provide lots of jobs for the area.
- The number of houses built in the area has grown steadily each year and I believe this is good for the town.
- I agree with the view of most local people that Inverdon Council is doing a good job for those who live in the area even though it faces financial difficulties.
- I am concerned about the number of migrant workers coming to Inverdon, and most local people share this view.
- Although wildlife tourists may be lost to the area, many more golf tourists will be attracted by the golf development.

Sally Anderson

- I am against the golf development because I believe that part of the course, if built according to plan, would be against the law.
- It is also clear that the vast majority of the public agree with my view that the golf development should not go ahead.
- Membership of the European Union allows people to travel to find work, and I think that migrant workers should be encouraged as they help our local economy.
- There are 300 homes to be built, but they are about 3 times more expensive than the average house in Inverdon, and few people will be able to afford them.
- Inverdon is a wealthy area, where people earn more than the Scottish average. I would much rather save our wild places than accept the jobs created by the golf development.

You must decide which option to recommend, **either** Ian McKay as the candidate (**Option 1**) **or** Sally Anderson as the candidate (**Option 2**).

(i)   Using Sources 1, 2 and 3 above, **which option would you choose**?

(ii) Give reasons to **support** your choice.

(iii) **Explain** why you did not choose the other option.

Your answer must be based on all three sources.   10

NOW GO TO SECTION 2 ON *PAGE NINE*

PART B — DEMOCRACY IN THE UNITED KINGDOM

In your answers to Questions 1 and 2 you should give recent examples from the United Kingdom.

Question 1

> Political Parties campaign to get their candidates elected as MPs.

Describe, **in detail**, **two** ways in which political parties campaign to get their candidates elected as MPs.

4

Question 2

> Some people want changes made to the House of Lords.

Explain, **in detail**, why some people want changes made to the House of Lords.

6

Part B (continued)

MARKS

Question 3

Study the Sources 1, 2 and 3 below, then attempt the question which follows.

You have been asked to recommend who should be your party's candidate for the constituency of Gleninch.

Option 1 Kirsty Reid	Option 2 Robbie McKay

SOURCE 1

Background Information about Gleninch Constituency

- Gleninch is a constituency in the north of Scotland with a population of 35,265 people. It is a largely rural area with only one town, Inverinch, and a large number of scattered villages. The traditional industries of farming and fishing have been in decline in recent years. The unemployment rate is well above the national average.
- Many young people leave the area, moving to the big cities throughout the UK to look for jobs or to attend college or university.
- Tourism is very important to the local economy, with a lot of people employed in hotels, bed and breakfast accommodation and restaurants. Tourists tend to visit the area for a few days on short breaks, attracted by rare wildlife and spectacular, unspoilt scenery. However, there are a number of transport problems in the constituency, including high petrol prices and poor public transport.
- There is a proposal to build a wind farm in the area. This would involve the construction of 6 large wind turbines along the coast, as well as a 15-mile long power line built on tall pylons to take electricity to the rest of the country. This would create a few temporary construction jobs but will disturb local wildlife and impact on the scenery of the area.
- An American mining company wants to build a huge "super quarry" into a mountainside near Gleninch. This will produce crushed rock to build roads, railways and houses throughout the UK. The new quarry will create 150 new jobs in Gleninch.
- At the last General Election, the constituency was won by the Labour Party with a majority of just over 1000 votes. The Liberal Democrats came second. They are convinced that, with the right candidate, they can win the seat at the next election.

A Statistical Profile of Gleninch Constituency (2013)

	Gleninch	Comparison with Scottish Average
Average Income	£21185	-14%
Income Support claimants	15.1%	+22%
Unemployment Rate	5.6%	+13%
School leavers with no qualifications	3.6%	-33%
School leavers with Highers	58.6%	+13%
Serious Assaults	8.8 (per 10 000 people)	-73%
Housebreaking	3.8 (per 10 000 people)	-93%
Road Accidents	57 casualties	-44%

Part B Question 3 (continued)

Survey of Local Liberal Democrat Members Question: *How important are these issues to people in the area?*				
Issue	Unimportant	Not Very Important	Fairly Important	Very Important
Environment	5%	25%	40%	30%
Health	2%	10%	53%	35%
Jobs	0%	0%	48%	52%
Women in Parliament	15%	52%	22%	11%

SOURCE 2

Extract from Campaign Speech by Kirsty Reid

- I support the proposed wind farm as it will provide many local jobs and help the local environment.
- Our local schools provide an excellent education. If selected, I will work to ensure this continues.
- Women make up over half the country's population and yet there are still very few of us who are MPs. This is a major priority for local party members and is an important reason why I should be the candidate.
- The local economy has been in decline recently. We need more jobs to keep our young people in the area. The new quarry will help with this, and I will work hard to see that it is allowed to go ahead.
- To attract more people to the area we need to improve transport links. I will make this a priority.

SOURCE 3

Extract from Campaign Speech by Robbie Mckay

- Tourism is very important to the area and so I will oppose the new wind farm as it will be an ugly blot on the landscape and deter tourists.
- Crime in Gleninch is among the worst in Scotland. I will campaign to improve policing in the area.
- Although new jobs are important, local Liberal Democrats are much more concerned about the environment. The new quarry will put more heavy lorries on our roads which are already more dangerous than the rest of the country. I will oppose it going ahead.
- The issue of health will be one of my main concerns, just as it is for local party members.
- Compared to the rest of the country, the people of Gleninch are not well off. I will do all I can to improve this.

You must decide which option to recommend, **either** Kirsty Reid as the candidate **(Option 1) or** Robbie McKay as the candidate **(Option 2)**.

(i)   Using Sources 1, 2 and 3 above and opposite, **which option would you choose?**

(ii) Give reasons to support your choice.

(iii) Explain why you did not choose the other option.

Your answer must be based on all three sources.

10

NOW GO TO SECTION 2 ON *PAGE NINE*

SECTION 2 — SOCIAL ISSUES IN THE UNITED KINGDOM — 20 marks

Attempt ONE part, either

Part C — Social Inequality   on pages 9–11

OR

Part D — Crime and the Law   on pages 12–14

PART C – SOCIAL INEQUALITY

In your answers to Questions 1 and 2 you should give recent examples from the United Kingdom.

Question 1

> The Government provides a range of financial benefits to help people in need.

Describe, **in detail**, at least two financial benefits provided by the Government which help people in need.

6

Question 2

> Health inequalities continue to exist in the UK.

Explain, **in detail**, why health inequalities continue to exist in the UK.

6

Part C (continued)

MARKS

Question 3

Study Sources 1, 2 and 3 below, then attempt the question which follows.

SOURCE 1

Families in Britain have changed over the years. More than 4 in 10 people over the age of 16 in the UK are married. In 2005, the average age for first marriage was 31 for men and 29 for women. This had been 26 and 23 for men and women respectively 40 years earlier. In 2005, the average age for divorce was 43 for men and 40 for women. This had been 39 and 37 for men and women respectively in 1995.

Marriages and Divorces in Britain

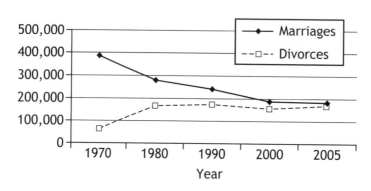

SOURCE 2

The total number of families reached 17 million in 2009. The "traditional" type of family has always been seen as a couple with dependent children. As the table shows, the percentage of families of each type in Britain has been changing. This may well have an impact on the welfare of dependent children. White people in Britain have the lowest percentage of married couples.

People in each type of household (%)

	1971	1981	1991	2009
One person	6	8	11	15
Couple no children	19	20	23	26
Couple with dependent children	52	47	41	35
Couple with non-dependent children only	10	10	11	9
Lone-parent family	4	6	10	13
Other households	9	9	4	2

Part C Question 3 (continued)

MARKS

SOURCE 3

Some 9% of people in Britain are non-white. Ethnic groups differ in terms of family size and type. 62% of white families are married couples, 13% are cohabiting couples and 25% are lone parent families. From 1970 to 2005 there has been a large drop in marriages in general but not in divorces.

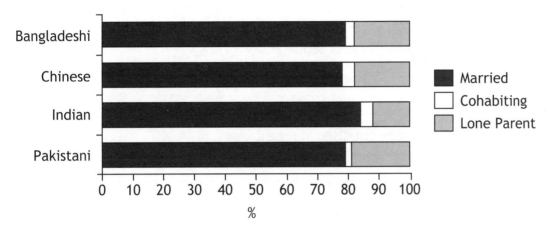

Using Sources 1, 2 and 3 above, what **conclusions** can be drawn about family life in the UK?

You should reach a conclusion about each of the following:

- changes in marriage and divorce in Britain

- the link between changes in marriages and changes in the "traditional" family

- the main difference between ethnic minority families and white families.

Your conclusion must be supported by evidence from the sources. You should link information within and between sources in support of your conclusions.

Your answer must be based on all three sources.

8

PART D – CRIME AND THE LAW

In your answers to Questions 1 and 2 you should give recent examples from the United Kingdom.

Question 1

Scotland has its own system of adult courts.

Describe, **in detail**, at least two adult courts in Scotland.

6

Question 2

The use of the prison system has been criticised in recent years.

Explain, **in detail**, why the use of the prison system has been criticised in recent years.

6

Part D (continued)

Question 3

Study Sources 1, 2 and 3 below and then attempt the question which follows.

SOURCE 1

The Scottish Government is considering a petition calling for a mandatory custodial sentence for any person found carrying a knife. This would mean that possession of such a weapon would automatically result in the offender being sent to prison or a detention centre. Community groups have called on the Government to take action to deter young people from carrying knives. Many members of the public believe that people should automatically be sent to jail, which would reduce crime – very few people think a fine would work. 1200 offenders were sentenced for possession of a knife between 2004 and 2009, but only 314 were given custodial sentences. Scottish Prisons reported that as a result of overcrowding, offenders were not serving their full sentence and were being released early. Automatic sentences may make this problem worse. In 2009, one in five people convicted of carrying a knife in Edinburgh had previously been charged for a similar offence. Some young people carry a knife for their own self-defence as they are worried about their personal safety when they go out. Thirty percent of young people thought that introducing tougher sentences would reduce knife crime.

Judges in Scotland think that they should be able to consider the personal circumstances of each case before sentencing. A custodial sentence can have a huge impact on the future of young people convicted. The number of people sent to prison for carrying a knife in public fell to a five-year low in 2008 because only one in three offenders were jailed. The threat of a custodial sentence may work as the number of murders with knives has decreased since 2003/2004.

SOURCE 2

Year	Total number of murders	Number of murders with knives
2003/2004	140	70
2004/2005	137	62
2005/2006	129	59
2006/2007	120	54
2007/2008	114	49

Results of Public Opinion Survey on Methods to Reduce Knife Crime

Automatic Jail Sentence	67%
Community Service	29%
Fine	4%

Part D Question 3 (continued)   MARKS | DO NOT WRITE IN THIS MARGIN

SOURCE 3

View of Maureen Andrew

We need to tackle knife crime which is a problem in many of our communities. People in my area are extremely worried and they are demanding that the penalties for carrying knives are much tougher. Many people won't leave their houses because they are frightened of young people roaming around in gangs. Many youths have stated that carrying a knife is part of being in a gang and they have to be seen to be armed – peer pressure is a key factor. We must send out a strong message to troublemakers who go out looking for a fight. Many of these individuals have been charged before, but this has had little effect on their behaviour. Young people have admitted that a jail sentence would make them think twice about carrying a knife.

Using Sources 1, 2 and 3 above, what **conclusions** can be drawn about knife crime in the UK?

You should reach a conclusion about each of the following:

- the rate of murders with knives

- reasons young people carry knives

- methods to reduce knife crime.

Your conclusions must be supported by evidence from the sources. You should link information within and between sources in support of your conclusions.

Your answer must be based on all three sources.   8

NOW GO TO SECTION 3 ON *PAGE FIFTEEN*

SECTION 3 — INTERNATIONAL ISSUES — 20 marks

Attempt ONE part, either

Part E — World Powers   on pages 15–17

OR

Part F — World Issues   on pages 18–21

PART E – WORLD POWERS

In your answers to Questions 1 and 2 you should give recent examples from a world power you have studied.

Question 1

> All governments respond to social and economic problems.

Describe, **in detail,** from a world power you have studied, at least two government's responses to social and economic problems.

6

Question 2

> Some citizens criticise their government for the limitations placed on their political rights.

Explain, **in detail**, why some citizens from a world power you have studied may criticise their government for the limitations placed on their political rights.

6

MARKS | DO NOT WRITE IN THIS MARGIN

Part E (continued)

Question 3

Study Sources 1, 2 and 3 below and then attempt the question which follows.

SOURCE 1

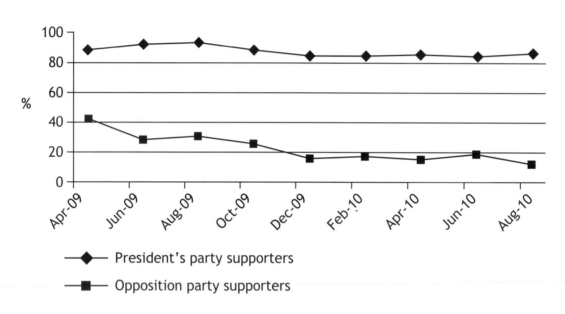

President of a G20 Country's Popularity Rating

—◆— President's party supporters

—■— Opposition party supporters

SOURCE 2

State	Question 1: For which party will you vote in the 2016 election? (%)		Question 2: At present, how good a job do you think the President is doing? (%)	
	President's Party	Opposition	A good job	A bad job
Alabama	45·9	39·5	49·1	42·9
Alaska	48·6	33·3	46·0	42·7
Hawaii	27·6	54·1	70·8	22·1
Idaho	49·7	34·6	46·3	43·7
Massachusetts	27·9	56·8	66·8	26·3
Rhode Island	24·5	56·2	66·6	26·3
Utah	51·9	31·0	47·8	40·8
Vermont	28·5	55·4	66·7	24·4
Wyoming	53·8	32·2	44·6	45·0

Part E Question 3 (continued)

SOURCE 3

The Ethnic Divide in the President's Popularity

As the President seeks re-election, a recent newspaper poll measured public opinion on the three main issues of the economy, terrorism and health. On the economy, 55% of Whites said they approved of the President's performance. Among Blacks, the figure was 91%. Thirty-six percent of Whites disapproved of the President's economic performance, while 2% of Blacks disapproved. Among Hispanics, 82% approved whilst the percentage of those disapproving was 10%. When asked if they were confident that the President could handle another major crisis, the different ethnic groups were also split. Fifty-five percent of Whites said they were confident, compared with 92% of Blacks and 83% Hispanics. When it came to the President's health reforms, the percentage of Whites in favour was 40%, whilst for Blacks it was 90% and 85% for Hispanics. Overall, nine out of ten Black and Hispanic Americans felt that the President cared about them while just over half of Whites shared this view. On each issue, a number of respondents had no view on the President's performance.

Using Sources 1, 2 and 3 explain why the view of Brad Simpson is **selective in the use of facts.**

The President remains popular, especially on the main issues for all ethnic groups and he remains popular especially amongst his own party.

View of Brad Simpson

In your answer you must:

give evidence from the sources that supports Brad Simpson's view

and

give evidence from the sources that opposes Brad Simpson's view.

Your answer must be based on all three sources.   8

PART F — WORLD ISSUES

In your answers to Questions 1 and 2 you should give recent examples from a world issue you have studied.

Question 1

International issues have many consequences.

Describe, **in detail,** at least two consequences of an international issue you have studied.

6

Question 2

International organisations work hard to try to resolve international issues or problems.

Explain, **in detail**, at least two ways in which international organisations try to resolve an international issue or problem you have studied.

6

Part F (continued)

Question 3

Study Sources 1, 2 and 3 below, then attempt the question which follows.

SOURCE 1

Adults (15–49) Living with HIV/Aids (%)

African country	2003	2008
Botswana	23·6	23·9
Ethiopia	4·3	2·1
Lesotho	23·5	23·2
Swaziland	32·5	26·1
Zimbabwe	22·1	15·3

Population Living in Poverty (%)

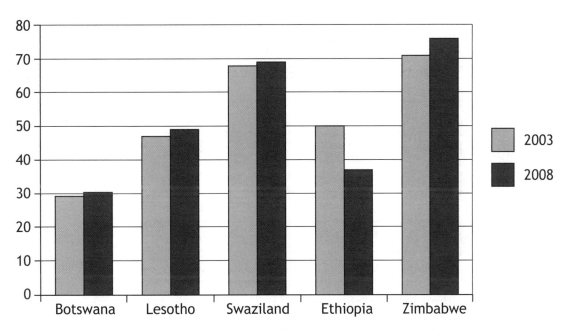

Part F Question 3 (continued)

SOURCE 2

Education — How well is Africa shaping up?

UNESCO is promising to help African countries through its "Literacy Decade" campaign. However, it points out that Africa has a long way to go, as one fifth of African adults are illiterate.

The economic crisis in Zimbabwe has had an effect on the education budget in recent years. They cannot find enough qualified teachers to work in their schools.

The government of Lesotho has shown a commitment to education. They spent 13% of their GDP on schooling in 2008 whilst, in 2003, it was 11%. This has had a positive effect on literacy rates.

In Botswana, literacy rates have changed from 80% to 84% since 2003. Every child in Botswana can expect to go to school for twelve years. Swaziland, a country badly affected by HIV/Aids, has seen literacy rates go from 74% in 2003 to 81% in 2008. The situation in Ethiopia mirrors much of Africa with literacy levels going up although they are still low when compared to developed countries.

SOURCE 3

Total Foreign Debt (Millions of US Dollars)

African country	2003	2008
Botswana	392	422
Ethiopia	4400	3100
Lesotho	507	619
Swaziland	357	554
Zimbabwe	3400	5300

Total Aid Received (Millions of US Dollars)

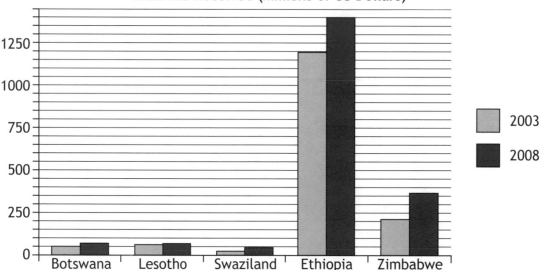

Page twenty

Part F Question 3 (continued)

Using Sources 1, 2 and 3 explain, in detail, why the view of Diane Lochrie is **selective in the use of facts.**

> **It is obvious that increasing aid reduces poverty in African countries and improves education, while those countries with increasing debt are unable to reduce the problem of HIV/AIDS.**
>
> **View of Diane Lochrie**

In your answer you must:

give evidence from the sources that supports Diane Lochrie's view

and

give evidence from the sources that opposes Diane Lochrie's view.

Your answer must be based on all three sources.   **8**

[END OF MODEL PAPER 2]

[BLANK PAGE]

Model Paper 3

Whilst this Model Paper has been specially commissioned by Hodder Gibson for use as practice for the National 5 exams, the key reference documents remain the SQA Specimen Paper 2013 and the SQA Past Papers 2014 and 2015.

National Qualifications
MODEL PAPER 3

Modern Studies

Duration — 1 hour and 30 minutes

Total marks — 60

SECTION 1 — DEMOCRACY IN SCOTLAND AND THE UNITED KINGDOM — 20 marks

Attempt ONE part, EITHER

SECTION 2 — SOCIAL ISSUES IN THE UNITED KINGDOM — 20 marks

Attempt ONE part, EITHER

SECTION 3 — INTERNATIONAL ISSUES — 20 marks

Attempt ONE part, EITHER

Before attempting the questions you must check that your answer booklet is for the same subject and level as this question paper.

Read the questions carefully.

On the answer booklet, you must clearly identify the question number you are attempting.

Use **blue** or **black** ink.

Before leaving the examination room you must give your answer booklet to the Invigilator.
If you do not, you may lose all the marks for this paper.

SECTION 1 — DEMOCRACY IN SCOTLAND AND THE UNITED KINGDOM — 20 marks

Attempt ONE part, either

Part A — Democracy in Scotland   on pages 2–4

OR

Part B — Democracy in the United Kingdom   on pages 5–7

PART A – DEMOCRACY IN SCOTLAND

In your answers to Questions 1 and 2 you should give recent examples from Scotland.

Question 1

> The First Minister has many powers in the Scottish Government.

Describe, **in detail,** at least two powers of the First Minister in the Scottish Government.

6

Question 2

> Since the Scottish Parliament Election in 2011, Scotland has been governed by a majority government.

Explain, **in detail**, why some people believe majority government works well AND explain, **in detail**, why some people believe majority government does not work well.

6

Part A (continued)

Question 3

Study Sources 1, 2 and 3, then attempt the question which follows.

SOURCE 1

Road Bridge Tolls Campaign

Following the Scottish Parliament election in May 2007, the Scottish National Party Government announced that it would abolish tolls on both the Forth and Tay Road Bridges. This announcement followed a long campaign led by a pressure group called the National Alliance Against Tolls (NAAT).

NAAT members took part in a campaign to have the bridge tolls removed. They lobbied local councillors, MSPs and MPs. NAAT also lobbied political parties and persuaded the Liberal Democrats to support the scrapping of bridge tolls. Members wrote hundreds of letters to newspapers; the group set up its own website; they used the 10 Downing Street e-petition set up by the Prime Minister and asked supporters to add their names. A by-election in Dunfermline, caused by the death of the serving Labour MP, was an opportunity for the group to increase their support and gain publicity when they put forward a candidate.

One newspaper, the Dundee Courier, strongly supported the campaign to abolish the tolls while another, The Herald, was not in favour of ending tolls on the bridges. Trade Unions were concerned about the impact on their members. Some local residents and the Green Party were worried about the increase in traffic and the impact upon the environment if tolls were scrapped. Many business groups, however, thought that the ending of tolls would benefit the economy of Scotland.

SOURCE 2

Result of Dunfermline & West Fife By-Election

Party	Candidate	Votes	%
Liberal Democrats	William Rennie	12,391	35.83%
Labour	Catherine Stihler	10,591	30.63%
Scottish National Party	Douglas Chapman	7,261	21.00%
Conservative & Unionist	Dr Carrie Ruxton	2,702	7.81%
Scottish Socialist Party	John McAllion	537	1.55%
Scottish Christian Party	Rev George Hargreaves	411	1.19%
Abolish Forth Bridge Tolls Party	Tom Minogue	374	1.08%
UKIP	Ian Borland	208	0.60%
Common Good	Rev Dr Dick Rogers	108	0.30%

Part A Question 3 (continued)

SOURCE 3

Selected Views on Bridge Tolls Campaign

Extracts from Statement by Tom Minogue (anti-toll by-election candidate):
Thank you to the people who voted for me . . . I consider that, taking all things into account, we have done well to poll 374 votes. It might not seem much but . . . this is no mean achievement when one considers that today marks the second week in existence for the Abolish Forth Bridge Tolls Party.

The NAAT website reported: for some reason, The Herald is still fighting to keep the tolls. This morning it published results of a poll of businesses, which included a question on removal of tolls. The result was that 58% of firms welcomed the removal of tolls yet The Herald says — *"The result falls short of being a ringing endorsement of a significant policy initiative."*

A Trade Union attacked the decision to scrap tolls on the Forth and Tay Bridges. The Transport and General Workers Union was concerned about job losses. It claimed the move will leave 175 of their members facing the loss of their jobs.

The Dundee Courier wrote: In the end it was all about people power. Tens of thousands of you backed The Courier's campaign to scrap tolls and make politicians act. It was a cause this paper believed could not be ignored and it was a cause our readers supported from the day we launched our campaign in March last year. By letter, phone or e-mail you said loud and clear "the tolls must go." Some 2000 of you added your signatures to the campaign in the first month, another 10,000 backed an online poll. Thousands more of you gave visible backing by displaying "Scrap The Tolls" stickers on your vehicles, taking the message with you wherever you travelled.

Using Sources 1, 2 and 3, explain why the view of Diana Jones is **selective in the use of facts.**

> The campaign to end the tolls on the Forth and Tay Bridges was successful and had the support of the people of Scotland.
>
> **View of Diana Jones**

In your answer you must:

give evidence from the sources that supports Diana Jones' view

and

give evidence from the sources that opposes Diana Jones' view.

Your answer must be based on all three sources.

8

NOW GO TO SECTION 2 ON *PAGE EIGHT*

PART B — DEMOCRACY IN THE UNITED KINGDOM

MARKS

In your answers to Questions 1 and 2 you should give recent examples from the United Kingdom.

Question 1

> The Prime Minister has many powers in the UK Government.

Describe, **in detail**, at least two powers of the Prime Minister in the UK Government.   6

Question 2

> Since the UK General Election in 2010, the UK has been governed by a coalition government.

Explain, **in detail**, why some people believe coalition government works well AND explain, **in detail**, why some people believe coalition government does not work well.   6

Part B (continued)

Question 3

Study Sources 1, 2 and 3 below, then attempt the question which follows.

SOURCE 1

Compulsory Voting

Election turnout has been falling in recent years and fewer people believe they have a duty to vote, leading to worries about the future of democracy in Britain. The Government is considering various ways to increase the number of people voting in elections. In the most recent UK General Election in 2010, turnout was 65%. This was a clear increase from the record low figure of 59.4% in 2001.

One suggestion has been to make voting compulsory. In the UK, compulsory voting is not part of electoral law. In a number of countries including Australia, Belgium, Greece and Brazil, voting is compulsory. Non-voters face a mixture of penalties, mainly fines. In Greece, turnout in elections is about 75% while in Australia in recent elections 95.4% of the electorate voted and of them, 4.8% spoiled their ballot paper.

Supporters of compulsory voting claim it increases turnout and so makes elections more democratic and representative of the views of voters. Parties do not have to worry about getting their supporters to vote and so can concentrate on the issues, leading to a better political debate.

Opponents of compulsory voting argue that having the right to vote also means having the right not to vote and it would be against British traditions to force reluctant voters to cast a vote. It would be difficult to enforce this law and would be a considerable waste of police and court time.

SOURCE 2

Survey of Public Opinion about Voting

Do you support making voting in elections compulsory?	
Yes	47%
No	49%
Don't Know	4%

Percentage of people over 18 who would definitely vote in a General Election, by age group

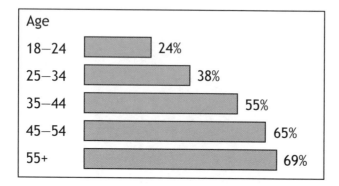

Age	
18–24	24%
25–34	38%
35–44	55%
45–54	65%
55+	69%

Part B Question 3 (continued)

MARKS | DO NOT WRITE IN THIS MARGIN

SOURCE 3

Selected Views on Compulsory Voting

- Brian Davidson MP said: "The introduction of compulsory voting is a way of getting people interested in politics, restoring a sense of community and confronting the issue of people who never vote."

- Oliver Heald MP said: "There is little support to make it a criminal offence not to vote . . . the police have better things to do. The challenge is for politicians to excite voters with their ideas."

- Forcing people to vote would not improve democracy in Britain. The reason why many people do not vote, especially young people, is that they do not think voting will make any difference and they do not have much trust in politicians. Forcing people into the polling booth would lead to a large number of spoiled ballot papers.

- Voting is a right and should be a duty. All citizens should participate in important decisions by voting. Ballot papers, however, should also have a space where voters can say "none of the above"; a high vote for none of the candidates will force politicians to pay more attention to the wishes of dissatisfied voters.

Using Sources 1, 2 and 3, explain why the view of Chris Knight is **selective in the use of facts**.

Compulsory voting would improve democracy and would be popular with voters.

View of Chris Knight

In your answer you must:

give evidence from the sources that supports Chris Knight's view

and

give evidence from the sources that opposes Chris Knight's view.

Your answer must be based on all three sources.

8

NOW GO TO SECTION 2 ON *PAGE EIGHT*

MARKS | DO NOT WRITE IN THIS MARGIN

SECTION 2 — SOCIAL ISSUES IN THE UNITED KINGDOM — 20 marks

Attempt ONE part, either

Part C — Social Inequality   on pages 8–11

OR

Part D — Crime and the Law   on pages 12–15

PART C – SOCIAL INEQUALITY

In your answers to Questions 1 and 2 you should give recent examples from the United Kingdom.

Question 1

Living in poverty has a big effect on children.

Describe, **in detail**, **two** effects of living in poverty on children.   **4**

Question 2

Health in Scotland can be improved by government policies and individual action.

Explain, **in detail,** the ways in which health in Scotland can be improved by government policies **and** individual actions.   **6**

Part C (continued)

Question 3

Study Sources 1, 2 and 3 below, then attempt the question which follows.

You are an adviser to the Scottish Government. You have been asked to recommend whether the Government should extend the scheme, which pays smokers to stop smoking, across the whole of Scotland, or to recommend scrapping the scheme.

Option 1	Option 2
Extend the scheme which pays smokers to stop smoking, across the whole of Scotland.	Scrap the scheme which pays smokers to stop smoking.

SOURCE 1

Facts and Viewpoints

The NHS in Dundee established a trial scheme in March 2009 which gives smokers financial incentives to give up cigarettes. The Scottish Government is considering whether to extend the scheme to the whole of Scotland.

Those on the scheme will have £12·50 credited onto an electronic card to buy groceries, if they pass a weekly breath test. The credits cannot be used to buy cigarettes or alcohol. Payments will be paid for a maximum of 12 weeks which will cost the NHS £150 per person.

There are 36,000 smokers in Dundee, about half of whom live in poverty. There are over 1 million smokers in Scotland, 43% of them live in poverty.

Some local people say it is unfair that smokers are getting extra money while others who live in poverty and don't smoke, get nothing.

It is hoped 1800 smokers will sign up for the project. The budget for the scheme is £540,000 over 2 years in Dundee. To extend the scheme across the whole of Scotland would cost £14 million.

Many NHS staff think that other methods such as nicotine gum are more effective in helping smokers to give up cigarettes.

After 3 months, 360 people had signed up to the project in Dundee.

The average cost to the NHS of nicotine replacements, such as patches and gum, is £800 per person.

Some experts believe that people need counselling to give up smoking.

Smoking-related illnesses cost the NHS in Scotland over £200 million per year.

Smokers spend an average of £51 per week on cigarettes. For those living in poverty, this is about 28% of their income.

Part C Question 3 (continued)

SOURCE 2

Success Rate of Selected Help to Stop Smoking

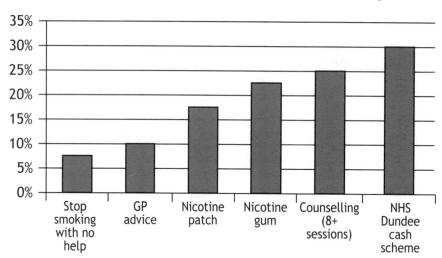

Percentage (%) Success Rate of Counselling in Stopping Smoking

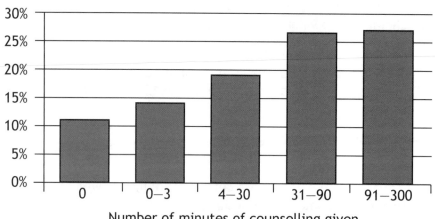

Number of minutes of counselling given

Part C Question 3 (continued)   MARKS | DO NOT WRITE IN THIS MARGIN

SOURCE 3

Viewpoints

Giving up smoking is the single most important lifestyle decision that smokers can make to improve their health and standard of living. Giving grocery money to smokers to help them quit has worked in Dundee. An extra £12·50 per week will help some of the poorest families to buy healthy food, which will also improve long-term health. Smoking-related illnesses cost the NHS millions of pounds every year and if we can get people to stop smoking using schemes like this, then it is money well worth spending. Those who quit will also save money every week through not buying cigarettes. This will make a huge difference to the income of families of ex-smokers.

Lewis McManus

Paying people to give up smoking will not work. It is unrealistic to expect people to give up for good after only 12 weeks. Alternatives such as nicotine gum and patches have proved to work in the long run. We should be encouraging people to go to long-term counselling, which has proven to be a very effective method. Although the cost of alternatives may seem higher, it will save the NHS a huge amount of money in the long run. Many non-smoking families are living in poverty, but they are not being paid £12·50 extra a week to help with their shopping. This scheme may even encourage people to start smoking to get grocery money.

Maria Logan

You must decide which option to recommend to the Scottish Government, **either** to extend the scheme which pays smokers to stop smoking, across the whole of Scotland **(Option 1)**, **or** to scrap the scheme which pays smokers to stop smoking **(Option 2)**.

(i)   Using Sources 1, 2 and 3 above, **which option would you choose**?

(ii) Give reasons to **support** your choice.

(iii) **Explain** why you did not make the other choice.

Your answer must be based on all three sources.   **10**

NOW GO TO SECTION 3 ON *PAGE SIXTEEN*

PART D – CRIME AND THE LAW

In your answers to Questions 1 and 2 you should give recent examples from the United Kingdom.

Question 1

> The work of the police in Scotland involves a variety of roles.

Describe, **in detail,** two roles of the police in Scotland.

4

Question 2

> Scottish courts often use alternative punishments to prison when dealing with offenders.

Explain, **in detail**, why Scottish courts often use alternative punishments to prison when dealing with offenders.

6

Part D (continued)

Question 3

Study Sources 1, 2 and 3 below, then attempt the question which follows.

You are an adviser to the Scottish Government. You have been asked to recommend whether the police should install more CCTV cameras or should not install more CCTV cameras.

Option 1	Option 2
Install more CCTV cameras.	Should not install more CCTV cameras.

SOURCE 1

Facts and Viewpoints

CCTV cameras were introduced to Scotland's streets as a method of tackling crime. There are now approximately 2,335 cameras in Scotland monitoring public spaces such as city centres, parks and shopping centres.

- CCTV is proven to be highly effective in reducing crime in some places, e.g. hospitals and car parks.

- Some research indicates where cameras are installed crime increases in nearby areas without CCTV cameras.

- Police believe that criminals are more likely to plead guilty when presented with CCTV evidence. This saves time in court and up to £5,000 of the costs of a trial.

- A case study in the Greater Glasgow area could find no link between the installation of CCTV cameras and a reduction in crime.

- Police officers report that one of their big frustrations is broken and vandalised cameras and CCTV images which do not capture offences clearly enough.

- There were 3,318 recorded incidents in 2008/9 using CCTV cameras which resulted in 587 evidence discs being provided for the Procurator Fiscal Service.

- Many members of the public are concerned that more CCTV means a loss of civil liberties and an invasion of their private lives.

- The majority of the public believe that the installation of more CCTV cameras is a positive thing.

- Scotland's cities already have too many cameras in operation compared to other countries, costing a huge amount of money.

- Strathclyde Police recently claimed a 75% drop in anti-social behaviour following the installation of a £130,000 CCTV system in a town with a history of this type of problem.

Part D Question 3 (continued)

SOURCE 2

Statistics by Area

	Crimes per year before CCTV installed	Crimes per year after CCTV installed	Percentage change
City	1,526	1,098	-20%
City car park	794	214	-73%
Hospital	18	12	-33%
Inner city estate	160	182	+14%

Public Feelings on Installation of CCTV Cameras

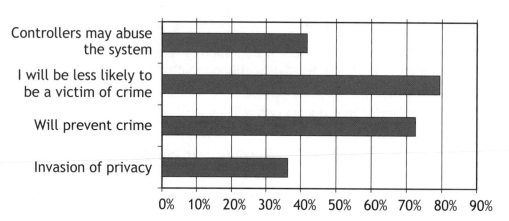

SOURCE 3

Viewpoints

Law-abiding citizens have nothing to fear from CCTV; in fact, it can help to protect them by deterring criminals from committing unlawful actions. CCTV can save taxpayers money by speeding up court cases. CCTV is of great benefit to police forces around the country, especially when dealing with anti-social behaviour. The CCTV operators can direct the police to any possible flashpoints so that they can deal with problems before they arise. In addition, if a crime is committed, the CCTV evidence can be used in court to identify a criminal. We should use more new technology to aid the fight against crime.

John Morton

Installing CCTV cameras does not reduce crime rates. CCTV cameras are not effective in solving even straightforward crimes like street robberies. One problem is that some operators have not been trained in using the system properly and as a result, the cameras can be badly positioned and out of focus. CCTV is an invasion of privacy as most ordinary citizens do not commit crime but still have their movements followed and recorded up to 300 times per day. At best, CCTV only makes offenders move away from areas with cameras to commit crimes where there are none. Too much money is wasted on CCTV cameras; this money would be better spent putting more police on the street.

Pauline Clark

You must decide which option to recommend to the Scottish Government, **either** they should install more CCTV cameras (**Option 1**) or should not install more CCTV cameras (**Option 2**).

Using Sources 1, 2 and 3 above, **which option would you choose**?

(i)　Give reasons to **support** your choice.

(ii)　**Explain** why you did not make the other choice.

Your answer must be based on all three sources.

10

NOW GO TO SECTION 3 ON *PAGE SIXTEEN*

SECTION 3 — INTERNATIONAL ISSUES — 20 marks

MARKS

Attempt ONE part, either

Part E — World Powers   on pages 16–19

OR

Part F — World Issues   on pages 20–23

PART E - WORLD POWERS

In your answers to Questions 1 and 2 you should give recent examples from a world power you have studied.

Question 1

> Citizens have many rights and responsibilities.

Describe, **in detail**, the rights and responsibilities of citizens from a world power you have studied.

6

Question 2

Social Problems Faced by World Powers

> Some groups experience social and economic inequalities.

Explain, **in detail**, why some groups from a world power you have studied experience social and economic inequality.

6

Part E (continued)

Question 3

Study Sources 1, 2 and 3 below, then attempt the question which follows.

SOURCE 1

Progress Made in Tackling HIV/AIDS

This G20 African country still has one of the worst death rates from HIV/AIDS and has the largest number of HIV-infected people in the world. At its peak in 2001 more than 20% of adults were infected with HIV and life expectancy fell from 60 years to 41 years. Since 2004, there has been a significant change in policies and programmes. On World AIDS Day, December 1 2009, the President stated his intention to get an HIV test and encouraged all the country's people to learn about their HIV status. The Government announced an increase in budget support for HIV/AIDS in 2010 to pay for the additional patients who will qualify for treatment under the new guidelines. Although the Government has made good progress in the treatment of HIV/AIDS, there are still major challenges as not all citizens get access to HIV prevention and treatments.

Progress has been made in the treatment of women and children. According to a UN report, the number of pregnant women receiving antiretroviral treatment (ART), which prevents mother-to-child transmission of HIV, almost doubled between 2010 and 2012. It also noted that ART is now available to over half of those in need, although provincial differences remain.

The UN report found that the Government's plan to tackle HIV/AIDS is one of the largest treatment coverage programmes in the world. As the country is ranked second in the world in terms of domestic spending on AIDS programmes. However, although there are signs that the HIV/AIDS epidemic has stabilised, the number of adults with HIV/AIDS remains high. Some Provinces have experienced higher rates of HIV/AIDS compared to others and this has reduced life expectancy in some Provinces.

SOURCE 2

Provincial Health Data 2012

Province	Percentage of deaths due to AIDS	Life expectancy (in years)	Percentage of HIV prevalence among children
Eastern Cape	43·2%	46	2·5%
Free State	52·5%	47	3·1%
Gauteng	55·7%	50	3·1%
KwaZulu Natal	57·9%	47	3·4%
Limpopo	42·7%	45	2·7%
Mpumalanga	56·3%	46	4·5%
Northern Cape	35·9%	53	1·9%
North West	54·2%	46	2·6%
Western Cape	28·5%	55	0·9%
Whole Country	**43·0%**	**49**	**2·5%**

Part E Question 3 (continued)

Treatment Gap: number of people who need antiretroviral treatment (ART) and those who are receiving ART, by Province

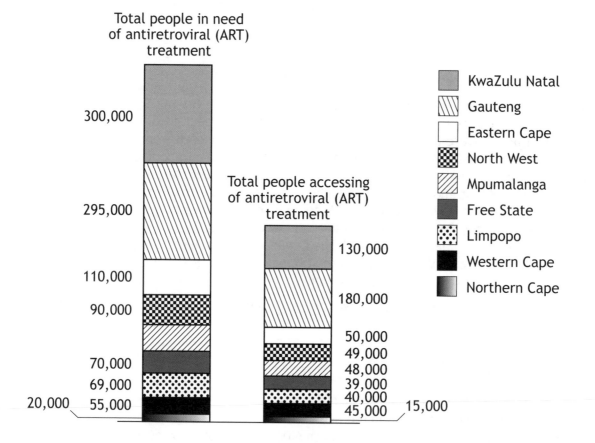

SOURCE 3

Year	Percentage of pregnant women who are HIV positive receiving antiretroviral (ART) treatment	Percentage of women attending antenatal clinics who are HIV positive
2004	15%	30%
2005	34%	30%
2006	52%	29%
2007	61%	28%
2008	73%	28%

MARKS | DO NOT WRITE IN THIS MARGIN

Part E Question 3 (continued)

Using Sources 1, 2 and 3 above, what **conclusions** can be drawn about HIV/AIDS in the country selected?

You should reach a conclusion about each of the following:

- HIV/AIDS in adults mothers and children

- provincial differences

- how effective the Government is in dealing with HIV/AIDS.

Your conclusions must be supported by evidence from the sources. You should link information within and between sources in support of your conclusions.   **8**

Your answer must be based on all three sources.

PART F — WORLD ISSUES

In your answers to Questions 1 and 2 you should give recent examples from a world issue you have studied.

Question 1

> The consequences of international issues impact on vulnerable groups.

Describe, **in detail**, at least two consequences of an international issue on vulnerable groups.

6

Question 2

> International issues or problems are difficult to resolve.

Explain, **in detail**, why it is difficult to resolve an international issue or problem you have studied.

6

Part F (continued)

Question 3

Study Sources 1, 2 and 3 below, then attempt the question which follows.

SOURCE 1

Terrorist Activity around the World in 2012

The international community has had some success in recent years in the battle against terrorism. This has resulted in the number of terrorist-related incidents worldwide dropping from a high in 2008 to a low in 2012. The amount of incidents in individual countries has also come down, with the amount in Afghanistan decreasing. However, the number of terrorist incidents in Somalia and Spain has increased, which is a worrying trend. In Somalia much has to be done to return the rule of law to society as the country is suffering from political and economic failure.

The motives for terrorist incidents varied from country to country. In Afghanistan, Pakistan and Somalia the most common motive for terror was religious reasons. This is due to Islamic extremism in these countries. In Spain nationalism was the main motive. The amount of deaths caused by terrorism remains very high even though the amount of terrorist incidents has dropped. More people died in a terrorist incident in Afghanistan than anywhere else, whereas the USA was the safest place from terrorism. In Pakistan a high number of deaths were caused by suicide attacks and car bombings.

SOURCE 2

Number of Terrorist Incidents Worldwide

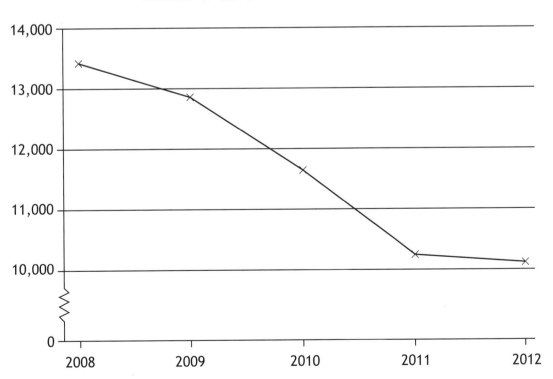

Part F (continued)

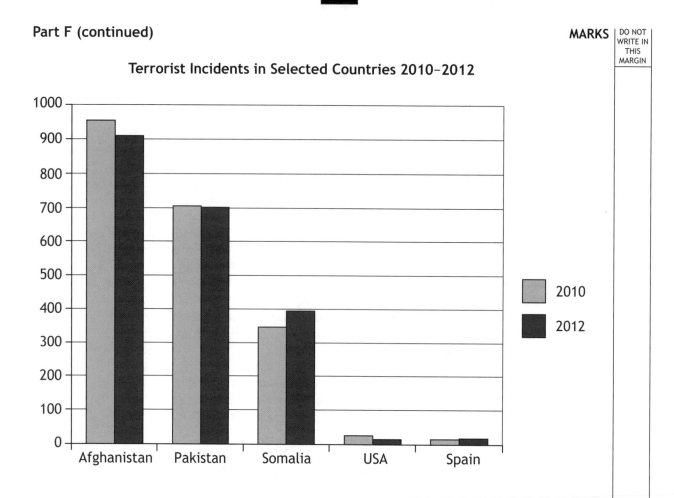

Terrorist Incidents in Selected Countries 2010–2012

Part F (continued)

SOURCE 3

Motives for Terrorist Incidents 2012

	Religion	Nationalism	Political	Other
Afghanistan	546	179	156	31
Pakistan	478	102	98	23
Somalia	125	80	91	2
USA	4	1	5	2
Spain	4	11	2	1

Deaths Caused by Terrorist Incidents 2012

Afghanistan	2193
Pakistan	1898
Somalia	1012
USA	8
Spain	11

Using Sources 1, 2 and 3, what **conclusions** can be drawn about terrorism around the world?

You should reach a conclusion about each of the following:

- changes in the level of terrorist incidents worldwide

- motives behind terrorist incidents in selected countries

- the levels of terrorist incidents in selected countries.

Your conclusions must be supported by evidence from the sources. You should link information within and between sources in support of your conclusions.

Your answer must be based on all three sources.

8

[END OF MODEL PAPER 3]

[BLANK PAGE]

NATIONAL 5

2014

National
Qualifications
2014

X749/75/01

Modern Studies

TUESDAY, 29 APRIL

9:00 AM – 10:30 AM

Total marks — 60

SECTION 1 — DEMOCRACY IN SCOTLAND AND THE UNITED KINGDOM — 20 marks

Attempt ONE part, EITHER

SECTION 2 — SOCIAL ISSUES IN THE UNITED KINGDOM — 20 marks

Attempt ONE part, EITHER

SECTION 3 — INTERNATIONAL ISSUES — 20 marks

Attempt ONE part, EITHER

Write your answers clearly in the answer booklet provided. In the answer booklet you must clearly identify the question number you are attempting.

Use **blue** or **black** ink.

Before leaving the examination room you must give your answer booklet to the Invigilator; if you do not, you may lose all the marks for this paper.

[BLANK PAGE]

SECTION 1 — DEMOCRACY IN SCOTLAND AND THE UNITED KINGDOM — 20 marks

Attempt ONE part, either

Part A— Democracy in Scotland   on pages 3–5

OR

Part B — Democracy in the United Kingdom   on pages 7–9

PART A— DEMOCRACY IN SCOTLAND

In your answers to Questions 1 and 2 you should give recent examples from Scotland.

Question 1

The Scottish Parliament has many devolved powers.

Describe, **in detail**, the devolved powers of the Scottish Parliament.   6

Question 2

Many people in Scotland choose to vote in elections.

Explain, **in detail**, why many people in Scotland choose to vote in elections.   6

[Turn over

PART A (continued)

Question 3

Study Sources 1, 2 and 3 then attempt the question which follows.

SOURCE 1

Scottish Parliament Election Factfile

Political parties have to keep detailed accounts of how much money they both receive and spend during elections. Political parties get their funding from a range of sources.

The Labour Party received approximately 36% of its donations at the 2011 election from the trade unions, whilst both the Conservatives and the SNP rely more on wealthy Scottish business people.

During the 2011 Scottish Parliament elections over £6·2 million was spent by the main political parties. This was however a drop from the £9·5 million spent in 2007.

A report on the 2011 Scottish Parliament election showed that most money was spent on campaign leaflets and letters from candidates. In 2007, the parties spent £1·2 million on these. In 2011, they spent £1·4 million.

In 2007, spending on advertising—such as billboards—was just over £1 million and £155,000 was spent on rallies and public meetings. In 2011, spending on advertising—such as billboards—was just over £438,600 and £47,000 was spent on rallies and public meetings.

In 2007, 22% of the public felt that there should be a ban on TV election broadcasts during elections. By 2011, this figure had fallen to 18%.

Voter awareness (%) of election campaign methods

Election	Received Leaflets	Noticed Billboard Advert	Attended a political meeting	Watched TV Broadcast
2007	89	62	3	70
2011	93	48	2	72

SOURCE 2

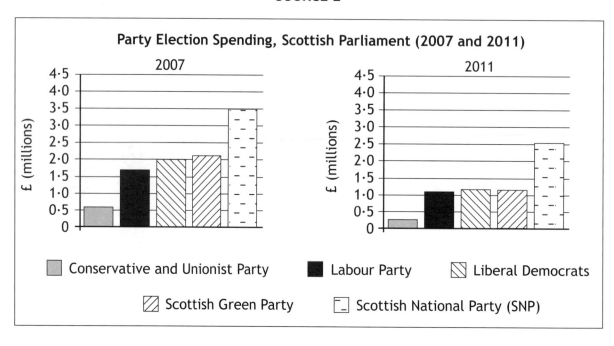

Page four

PART A Question 3 (continued)

SOURCE 3

Scottish Parliament Election Results (number of MSPs)

	Conservative	Labour	Liberal Democrats	SNP
2007	17	46	16	47
2011	15	37	5	69

The source of donations to all political parties (2011)

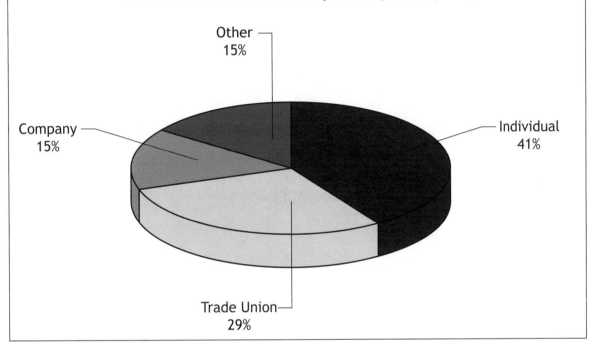

Other 15%
Company 15%
Individual 41%
Trade Union 29%

Using Sources 1, 2 and 3 what **conclusions** can be drawn about recent Scottish Parliament elections?

You should reach a conclusion about **each** of the following.

- The importance of trade union donations to the party election campaigns.
- The link between a party's election spending and election success.
- The link between election spending and voter awareness of election campaign methods.

Your conclusions **must** be supported by evidence from the sources. You should link information within and between the sources in support of your conclusions.

Your answer **must** be based on all three sources.

8

NOW GO TO SECTION 2 ON *PAGE ELEVEN*

[BLANK PAGE]

PART B — DEMOCRACY IN THE UNITED KINGDOM

In your answers to Questions 1 and 2 you should give recent examples from the United Kingdom.

Question 1

The UK Parliament has many reserved powers in Scotland.

Describe, **in detail**, the reserved powers of the UK Parliament in Scotland.   **6**

Question 2

Many people in the UK choose to vote in elections.

Explain, **in detail**, why many people in the UK choose to vote in elections.   **6**

[Turn over

PART B (continued)

Question 3

Study Sources 1, 2 and 3 then attempt the question which follows.

SOURCE 1

UK General Election Factfile

Political parties have to keep detailed accounts of how much money they both receive and spend during elections. Political parties get their funding from a range of sources.

During the 2010 UK General Election ten parties reported receiving donations and loans totalling over £14 million. Many small parties however did not receive any money. The Labour Party received approximately 36% of its donations from trade unions in 2009 whilst the Conservatives and the Liberal Democrats relied more on donations from rich business individuals.

A report on the 2010 UK General Election showed that most money was spent on campaign leaflets and other materials such as letters from candidates. In 2005, the parties spent £8·9 million on these. In 2010, they spent £12·3 million.

In 2010, spending on advertising — such as billboards — was £9 million and £1·7 million was spent on rallies and public meetings. In 2005, spending on advertising — such as billboards — was £15 million and £4·1 million was spent on rallies and public meetings.

In 2005, 22% of the public felt that there should be a ban on TV election broadcasts during general elections. By 2010, this figure had fallen to 18%.

UK public's awareness (%) of election campaigns

Election	Received Leaflets (%)	Noticed Billboard Advert (%)	Attended a political meeting (%)	Watched TV Broadcast (%)
2005	89	62	4	70
2010	93	48	2	72

SOURCE 2

UK Political Party Spending in 2005 and 2010

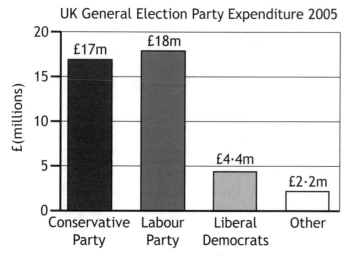

UK General Election Party Expenditure 2005

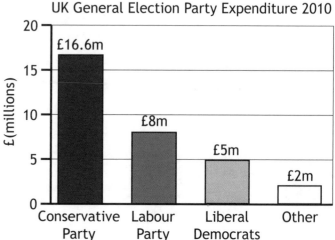

UK General Election Party Expenditure 2010

PART B Question 3 (continued)

SOURCE 3

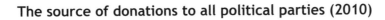

UK General Election Results (number of MPs)

	Conservative	Labour	Liberal Democrats	Others
2010	307	258	57	28
2005	198	356	62	30
2001	166	413	52	28

The source of donations to all political parties (2010)

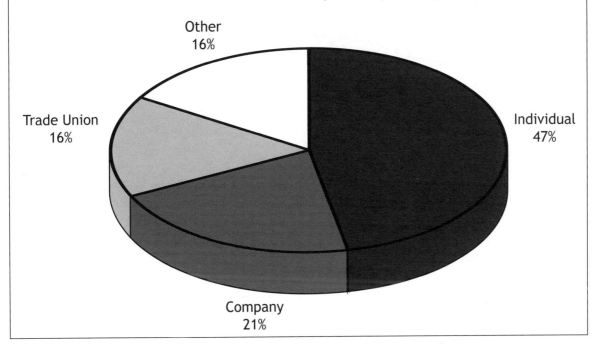

Using Sources 1, 2 and 3 what **conclusions** can be drawn about recent UK general elections?

You should reach a conclusion about **each** of the following.

- The importance of trade union donations to the party election campaigns.
- The link between a party's election spending and election success.
- The link between election spending and voter awareness of election campaign methods.

Your conclusions **must** be supported by evidence from the sources. You should link information within and between the sources in support of your conclusions.

Your answer **must** be based on all three sources.

8

NOW GO TO SECTION 2 ON *PAGE ELEVEN*

[BLANK PAGE]

SECTION 2 — SOCIAL ISSUES IN THE UNITED KINGDOM — 20 marks

Attempt ONE part, either

Part C — Social Inequality   on pages 11–13

OR

Part D — Crime and the Law   on pages 15–17

PART C — SOCIAL INEQUALITY

In your answers to Questions 1 and 2 you should give recent examples from the United Kingdom.

Question 1

Groups that tackle inequality in the UK			
Government	Individuals	Voluntary sector	Private sector

Choose **one** of the groups above.

Describe, **in detail, two** ways in which the group you have chosen has tried to tackle inequality in the UK.

4

Question 2

> Some people in the UK live in poverty, while others do not.

Explain, **in detail**, why some people in the UK live in poverty.

8

[Turn over

PART C (continued)

Question 3

Study Sources 1, 2 and 3 then attempt the question which follows.

SOURCE 1

The Daily Times

We May Be Fat But We're Healthier Than Ever

People in the UK are living longer than ever before despite concerns about health problems such as smoking and obesity (being significantly overweight). Average life expectancy in 2003 was 77 years. In 2013, it was 80 years. However the UK's life expectancy still compares poorly with other European countries.

Life expectancy in the UK has increased because we are making better lifestyle choices about our health, such as eating healthier food and exercising more. Life expectancy in the UK has also increased because of the good work of the NHS such as improvements in treating heart disease and cancers and Government policies such as anti-smoking laws. This has helped the UK reduce death rates from heart disease more than any other European country.

Many doctors warn that more has to be done to tackle the growing problem of childhood obesity and the health problems it causes. Since 2004, the number of obese children suffering from diabetes has doubled. If studies are accurate half of all adults in the UK will be obese by 2030.

SOURCE 2

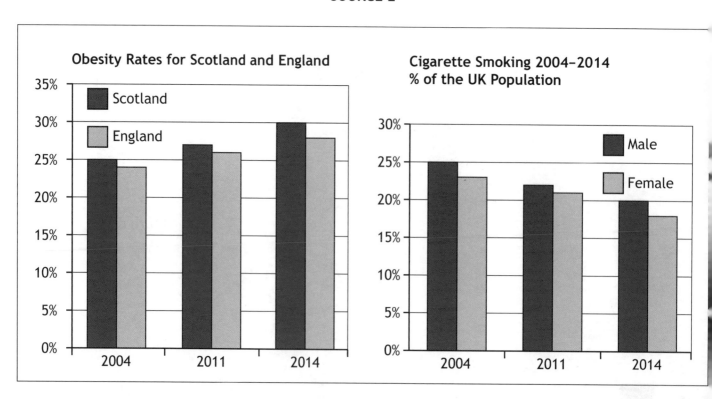

PART C Question 3 (continued)

SOURCE 3

Government Action to Reduce Smoking

The Government has worked hard to tackle the health problems associated with the issue of smoking. The Scottish Government banned smoking in public places in 2006. Since then the number of adults smoking has fallen, leading to a reduction in smoking related illness. England's smoke free laws came into effect one year later.

One study has found that the number of hospital admissions for children with asthma has gone from 26,969 cases in 2006 to 20,167 cases in 2013. Likewise, the number of hospital admissions for heart attacks linked to smoking has decreased.

Despite these improvements, one in five adults continues to smoke even though they know it is bad for their health. The highest rates of smoking in the UK are in Scotland with 27% of the adult population continuing to smoke. Smoking rates are also much higher within deprived inner city areas where rates have remained at 40% for the last 10 years.

Using Sources 1, 2 and 3, explain why the view of Sophie Wilson **is selective in the use of facts**.

There have been great improvements in the UK's health in the last 10 years.

View of Sophie Wilson

In your answer you **must**:

- give evidence from the sources that supports Sophie Wilson's view

and

- give evidence from the sources that opposes Sophie Wilson's view.

Your answer **must** be based on all three sources.   8

NOW GO TO SECTION 3 ON *PAGE NINETEEN*

[BLANK PAGE]

PART D — CRIME AND THE LAW

In your answers to Questions 1 and 2 you should give recent examples from the United Kingdom.

Question 1

> The Children's Hearing System can help young people in Scotland in different ways.

Describe, **in detail, two** ways that the Children's Hearing System can help young people in Scotland.

4

Question 2

> Other punishments are increasingly being used as alternatives to prison sentences in the UK.

Explain, **in detail**, why other punishments are being used as alternatives to prison sentences in the UK.

8

[Turn over

PART D (continued)

Question 3

Study Sources 1, 2 and 3 then attempt the question which follows.

SOURCE 1

Facts and Viewpoints

The Victims and Witnesses (Scotland) Bill was introduced in 2013 by the Scottish Government and was intended to make sure that all victims and witnesses are guaranteed certain rights by law.

- The Victims and Witnesses Bill, proposes a "victim surcharge", meaning that those who commit crimes will contribute to the cost of providing support to victims eg house alarm systems and travel costs to hospital.

- Victim Support Scotland (VSS) is a voluntary group which provides a listening service for victims. Their volunteers can be easily contacted by phone, email or face to face.

- Victim Support volunteers are not trained counsellors and can only give practical information.

- Over £5 million per year is provided by the Scottish Government to support VSS and it has committed to maintaining that level of funding.

- Surveys show that victims are satisfied with the help and support given to them as victims of crime.

- The VSS run the Scottish Victim Crisis Centre (SVCC) but funding is so low that victims often get an engaged tone or an answering machine.

- The SVCC has a 9 month waiting list for victims who wish to talk about their experiences of crime.

- The Scottish Government give the SVCC £50,000 a year but staff say this is nowhere near enough to meet the demand for their services.

SOURCE 2

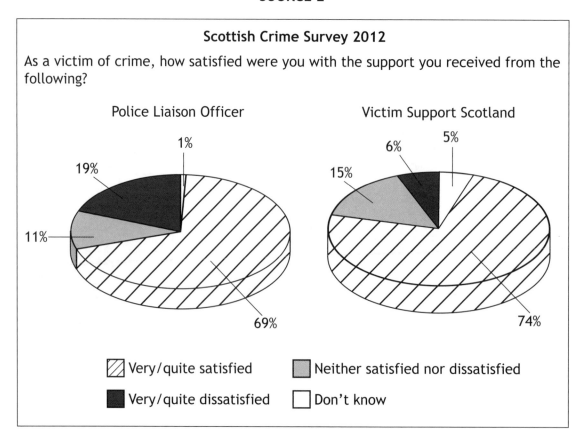

Scottish Crime Survey 2012

As a victim of crime, how satisfied were you with the support you received from the following?

Police Liaison Officer

1%
19%
11%
69%

Victim Support Scotland

6% 5%
15%
74%

▨ Very/quite satisfied   ▢ Neither satisfied nor dissatisfied

◼ Very/quite dissatisfied   ☐ Don't know

PART D Question 3 (continued)

SOURCE 3

Statement by a Victim Support Campaigner

The Scottish Government has made a very positive attempt to support victims of crime in introducing the Victim and Witness Bill. They have clearly listened to what victims want and have introduced the victim surcharge which financially supports victims of crime. Victims on the whole are happy with the support they get from voluntary groups and the police. However, the funding given to some voluntary groups is simply not enough to support the level of demand for services such as counselling and advice. Some voluntary groups are not able to give full training to their staff as they can't afford it.

Using Sources 1, 2 and 3 explain why the view of Oliver Thomson **is selective in the use of facts.**

Victims of crime in Scotland receive satisfactory support.

View of Oliver Thomson

In your answer you **must:**

- give evidence from the sources that supports Oliver Thomson's view

and

- give evidence from the sources that opposes Oliver Thomson's view.

Your answer **must** be based on all three sources.

8

NOW GO TO SECTION 3 ON *PAGE NINETEEN*

[BLANK PAGE]

SECTION 3 — INTERNATIONAL ISSUES — 20 marks

Attempt ONE part, either

Part E — World Powers   on pages 19–21

OR

Part F — World Issues   on pages 23–25

PART E — WORLD POWERS

In your answers to Questions 1 and 2 you should give recent examples from a world power you have studied.

Question 1

> Governments have made many attempts to tackle social and economic inequality.

Describe, **in detail**, **two** ways in which the government of the world power you have studied has tried to tackle social and economic inequality.   4

Question 2

> Some groups of people are more likely to participate in politics than others.

Explain, **in detail**, why some groups of people in the world power you have studied are more likely to participate in politics than others.   6

[Turn over

Page nineteen

PART E (continued)

Question 3

Study Sources 1, 2 and 3 then attempt the question which follows.

You are a government adviser. You have been asked to recommend **whether or not** the Government of Australia should abolish compulsory voting.

Option 1	**Option 2**
Keep compulsory voting in Australia	Get rid of compulsory voting in Australia

SOURCE 1

Compulsory Voting

Most democratic governments consider voting in elections to be a right for all their citizens.

In Australia the government go further and punish those who do not vote with a fine. Voting in Australian elections is compulsory by law.

Australia has had some form of compulsory voting since the early 1900s and it is widely supported by Australian people. If you do not vote, you are fined $20 as punishment. You can be excused from voting if you provide a "valid and sufficient" reason eg serious illness.

Voter turnout in Australia was 47% prior to the 1924 compulsory voting law. In the decades since 1924, voter turnout has hovered around 95%.

In Australia 84% of people say they take voting seriously. However, 37% think a fine for not voting is fair. 9% of Australians admit to having at some time registered an informal vote (deliberately spoiling their paper).

Some suggest that it is undemocratic to force people to vote as it is against their right to freedom of choice. Opponents of compulsory voting argue that people with little interest in politics are forced to the polls; this increases the number of "informal votes". In addition, millions of dollars are spent on checking up on those who didn't turn out to vote.

SOURCE 2

Recent Election Statistics From Selected G20 Countries			
		Turnout (%)	Informal votes (%)
Countries with compulsory voting	Argentina	79·39	4·48
	Australia	93·22	5·6
	Brazil	81·88	8·64
Countries without compulsory voting	Canada	61·41	0·7
	Germany	70·78	1·44
	Russia	60·10	1·57

PART E Question 3 (continued)

SOURCE 3

Aussie News online: Compulsory voting could be scrapped

There is a possibility that nearly a century of compulsory voting will come to an end. Some politicians have recommended that it should be abolished. The Prime Minister of Australia wants to keep compulsory voting, despite calls to reform the election rules.

In the state of Queensland alone, about 250,000 people — roughly 8% of the roll — failed to vote in the last state election. Almost $1 million in state funds has been allocated to chase up those who failed to vote.

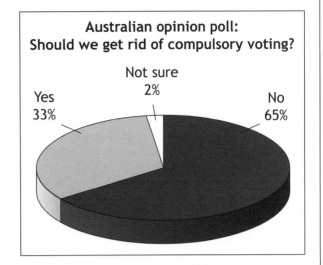

Australian opinion poll: Should we get rid of compulsory voting?

Not sure 2%
Yes 33%
No 65%

Have Your Say

Nic-C from Wilsonton	4 days ago

Forcing Australian citizens to vote is wrong. Everyone should have the right not to vote.

Ray Sunshine from Camp Hill	5 days ago

It's a privilege to vote. Compared to other countries, turnout here is much better so the results are more accurate.

Bruce T from Toowoomba South	5 days ago

People need to vote and not be lazy, but poor people don't have a way to get to their voting place unlike rich people who have cars.

Eileen Smith from Darling Heights	1 week ago

Forcing the population to vote means they will just deliberately spoil their ballot papers to avoid a fine.

Eddie from Ipswich	2 weeks ago

People who aren't interested should not be required to vote — bad decisions in the voting booth contribute to bad government.

Iain Thorpe from Mentone	2 months ago

When the turnout is low it means that a minority of society decide who the government is. I agree with most Australians who think we should keep compulsory voting.

You **must** decide which option to recommend, **either** keep compulsory voting in Australia (Option 1) **or** get rid of compulsory voting in Australia (Option 2).

(i) Using Sources 1, 2 and 3 **which option would you choose?**

(ii) Give reasons to **support** your choice.

(iii) **Explain** why you did not choose the other option.

Your answer **must** be based on all three sources.

10

[Turn over

[BLANK PAGE]

PART F — WORLD ISSUES

In your answers to Questions 1 and 2 you should give recent examples from a world issue you have studied.

Question 1

> International organisations often try to resolve conflicts or issues without using military force.

Describe, **in detail**, **two** ways in which international organisations have tried to resolve a conflict **or** issue without using military force.   **4**

Question 2

> There are many factors which cause international conflicts and issues.

Explain, **in detail**, the factors which caused an international conflict **or** issue you have studied.   **6**

[Turn over

PART F (continued)

Question 3

Study Sources 1, 2 and 3 then attempt the question which follows.

You are a military adviser working for the North Atlantic Treaty Organisation (NATO) which is a military alliance. This is made up of the USA, UK and twenty six other Western countries.

You have been asked to recommend **whether or not** NATO should send in troops to stop the civil war in Country A.

Option 1: Send NATO troops to Country A	Option 2: Do not send NATO troops to Country A

SOURCE 1

Country A—Conflict in the Middle East

The conflict in Country A began as a series of huge anti-government demonstrations in early 2011. These protests became increasingly violent. Many hundreds of protestors were arrested, beaten, tortured and killed.

Country A's President had never tolerated any criticism of his Government by the people and free elections were never held. The media was also completely controlled by the President. Most of the people believe that democratic reform, fair elections and a free media are needed in Country A.

Protests soon escalated into a full-scale civil war. The rebel army announced its formation in July 2011 and mounted attacks on government targets. The United Nations estimate that so far, 140 000 people have been killed and that many of them were civilians, killed by the President's troops.

The rebel army had some success against the President's troops. Many Western governments gave the rebels weapons, equipment and money. The UK and the USA especially wanted to replace the President with a much friendlier government.

Many in the rebel army have been calling for the West to send in troops to help them defeat the "tyrant" President. Feelings are running high after reports that his Government troops used chemical weapons to kill over 600 civilians in an area controlled by the rebel army. However, many observers think that more armed troops would only make matters worse.

SOURCE 2

Public opinion poll
(Conducted in all 28 NATO countries — 10 000 citizens)

How strongly do you **agree or disagree** with the following statements?

	Strongly disagree (%)	Disagree (%)	Agree (%)	Strongly agree (%)
NATO should send troops to Country A	54	18	16	12
NATO cannot afford to send troops to Country A	12	19	27	42
More armed foreigners will make things worse	8	21	29	42
NATO troops wouldn't help the refugees	6	11	30	53
NATO must do everything to stop chemical weapons	6	9	35	50
NATO needs friendly Middle Eastern governments	15	26	20	39

PART F Question 3 (continued)

SOURCE 3

NATO News online: Troops in Country A?

NATO members are considering sending almost 100,000 troops to try to stop the fighting in Country A. This would be a huge step for NATO. Although NATO did use air power to help overthrow Gaddafi in Libya in 2011, this would be the first time NATO ground troops have ever been used outside Europe. The loss of life among NATO forces could be extremely high. Many NATO governments are very worried about the massive cost of such an operation.

Have Your Say

George-M from London   6 hours ago
The intervention in Libya cost the UK and USA 21·5 billion dollars and that didn't involve ground troops!

David-W from New York   12 hours ago
We cannot stand by and watch this President kill his own people with chemical weapons. NATO got rid of Gaddafi in Libya.

Katriona-N from Berlin   yesterday
Sending more foreigners with guns into Country A will just make things worse. There are enough men with guns already.

Karen-F from Madrid   3 days ago
Almost two million refugees have fled the country and are living in terrible conditions in stinking refugee camps. Neighbouring countries cannot cope any longer.

Andy-N from Rome   last week
The people of Country A have been lied to for too long by the President. Democracy is what they need.

Vikki-D from Liverpool   last month
Refugees desperately need help, not guns and bombs. Our governments mustn't sacrifice any more of our young soldiers.

You **must** decide which option to recommend, **either** send NATO troops to Country A (Option 1) **or** do not send NATO troops to Country A (Option 2).

    (i) Using Sources 1, 2 and 3 **which option would you choose?**

    (ii) Give reasons to **support** your choice.

    (iii) **Explain** why you did not choose the other option.

Your answer **must** be based on all three sources.   10

[END OF QUESTION PAPER]

[BLANK PAGE]

NATIONAL 5

2015

National Qualifications 2015

X749/75/11

Modern Studies

WEDNESDAY, 27 MAY

9:00 AM – 10:45 AM

Total marks — 60

SECTION 1 — DEMOCRACY IN SCOTLAND AND THE UNITED KINGDOM — 20 marks

Attempt ONE part, EITHER

SECTION 2 — SOCIAL ISSUES IN THE UNITED KINGDOM — 20 marks

Attempt ONE part, EITHER

SECTION 3 — INTERNATIONAL ISSUES — 20 marks

Attempt ONE part, EITHER

Write your answers clearly in the answer booklet provided. In the answer booklet you must clearly identify the question number you are attempting.

Use **blue** or **black** ink.

Before leaving the examination room you must give your answer booklet to the Invigilator; if you do not, you may lose all the marks for this paper.

MARKS

SECTION 1 — DEMOCRACY IN SCOTLAND AND THE UNITED KINGDOM — 20 marks

Attempt ONE part, either

Part A— Democracy in Scotland   on pages 2–5

OR

Part B— Democracy in the United Kingdom   on pages 6–9

PART A— DEMOCRACY IN SCOTLAND

In your answers to Questions 1 and 2 you should give recent examples from Scotland.

Question 1

> Local councils provide many services in Scotland.

Describe, **in detail**, **two** services provided by local councils in Scotland.   4

Question 2

> People in Scotland can participate in society in many ways.

Explain, **in detail**, why some people participate in **one** of the following:

- Pressure Groups
- Trade Unions
- The Media.   6

[Turn over for Question 3 on *Page four*

DO NOT WRITE ON THIS PAGE

PART A (continued)

Question 3

Study Sources 1, 2 and 3 and then answer the question which follows.

Glenlochy is about to elect a new MSP. You are a voter in Glenlochy. You are undecided between Option 1 and Option 2.

Using sources 1, 2 and 3 you must decide which option to choose.

Option 1
Daisy Frost, candidate for the Scottish Labour Party

Option 2
Tom Kirk, candidate for the Scottish National Party

SOURCE 1

BestPals   🏠 Home   ⚙ Settings   ▼ | Search   🔍

Daisy Frost

Age 56

Studied Politics at Abertay University

Currently a local councillor

If I am elected to represent Glenlochy I will work to ensure that more women are elected to the Scottish Parliament. I believe that the lack of women in Holyrood has affected the number of women working locally. This needs to change.

Unemployment is clearly a problem in the local area and I would work hard to increase job opportunities. A lack of internet access is an obvious barrier and I would seek to improve this.

Crime is not a major concern so I would not focus on this if elected but would try to increase access to childcare as this is important to the community. Health care is an area I am passionate about and health in Glenlochy needs to improve. The lives of the people of Glenlochy are being cruelly cut short and I pledge to change this.

Tom Kirk

Age 35

Studied Law at Aberdeen University

Currently a lawyer for Citizens' Advice

Employment is a key area which I will try to improve if elected. Too few local people are in full-time work. This means that too many are also relying on benefits to get by.

I will work hard to ensure that the elderly of Glenlochy continue to be treated with dignity and feel safe in the local community. The majority of local people agree with me that elderly people are well cared for.

Skills education is key to any improvements in Glenlochy. Unfortunately at the moment too many local children are leaving school before S6 without the skills they need.

Childcare is not a major concern so I would not focus on this if elected but would try to decrease crime as this is a major concern in the community.

PART A Question 3 (continued)   MARKS

SOURCE 2

Selected Facts about Glenlochy

Glenlochy is a constituency for the Scottish Parliament in central Scotland. This part of Scotland used to rely on coal mining as its main industry. There is now only one major employer, a call centre in the main town of Glenlochy. Last month it made 100 full time workers redundant. Parts of the area are amongst the most deprived in Scotland and there are few job opportunities. Average life expectancy in the area is 77 compared to a Scottish average of 79.

Glenlochy Constituency is holding a by-election due to the death of the previous MSP. Many people feel the area now needs an experienced representative.

There was a local meeting about crime levels last month in the town hall where 530 residents turned up to speak to the local community police officer about their concerns. Carol Fife, Chair of the Community Council said "Crime is clearly increasing. We are very worried about this issue. Our new MSP needs to have a legal background".

Opinion Poll of 1000 Glenlochy Residents

	The elderly are well looked after in Glenlochy	Crime is a problem in Glenlochy	The Scottish Parliament needs more female MSPs	A lack of childcare is a major problem locally
Strongly agree	12%	30%	21%	36%
Agree	23%	35%	33%	32%
Disagree	25%	26%	25%	22%
Strongly disagree	40%	9%	21%	10%

SOURCE 3

Glenlochy Statistics (%)

	Glenlochy	Scotland
Unemployed and seeking work	9	7
Claiming benefits	17·5	15·8
Full time employment	42	48
Women in work	34	45
Suffering long term ill health	15	18
Pupils completing S6 at school	56	54
Households with internet access	79	76

You must decide which option to recommend, **either** Daisy Frost (**Option 1**) **or** Tom Kirk (**Option 2**).

(i)   Using Sources 1, 2 and 3, **which option would you choose?**

(ii)   Give reasons to **support** your choice.

(iii)   **Explain** why you did not choose the other option.

Your answer **must** be based on all three sources.   10

NOW GO TO SECTION 2 ON *PAGE TEN*

MARKS

PART B — DEMOCRACY IN THE UNITED KINGDOM

In your answers to Questions 4 and 5 you should give recent examples from the United Kingdom.

Question 4

> The House of Lords has an important role in the UK Government.

Describe, **in detail**, **two** of the roles the House of Lords has in the UK Government.   4

Question 5

> People in the UK can participate in society in many ways.

Explain, **in detail**, why some people participate in **one** of the following:

- Pressure Groups
- Trade Unions
- The Media.   6

[Turn over for Question 6 on *Page eight*

DO NOT WRITE ON THIS PAGE

PART B (continued)

Question 6

Study Sources 1, 2 and 3 and then answer the question which follows.

Millwood is about to elect a new MP. You are a voter in Millwood. You are undecided between Option 1 and Option 2

Using sources 1, 2 and 3 you must decide which option to choose.

Option 1	**Option 2**
Nora Manson, candidate for the Scottish Conservative Party	John Donaldson, candidate for the Scottish Liberal Democratic Party

SOURCE 1

BestPals   🏠 **Home**   ⚙ **Settings**   ▼ | Search | 🔍 |

Nora Manson
Age 56
Studied Politics at Glasgow University
Currently a local councillor
Born in Millwood

John Donaldson
Age 35
Studied Law at Edinburgh University
Currently a lawyer for Citizens' Advice
Born in Millwood

If I am elected to represent Millwood I will work to ensure that more women are elected to the UK parliament. I believe that the lack of women in Westminster has an effect on the number of women working locally. This needs to change.

Unemployment is clearly a problem in the local area and I would work hard to increase job opportunities. A lack of internet access is an obvious barrier and I would seek to improve this.

Crime is not a major concern so I would not focus on this if elected but would try to increase access to childcare as this is important to the community. Health care is an area I am passionate about and health in Millwood needs to improve. The lives of the people of Millwood are being cruelly cut short and I pledge to change this.

Employment is a key area which I will try to improve if elected. Too few local people are in full-time work. This means that too many are also relying on benefits to get by.

I will work hard to ensure that the elderly of Millwood are treated with dignity and feel safe in the local community. The majority of local people agree with me that elderly people are well cared for.

Skills education is vital if improvements are to be made. At the moment too many local children are leaving school before S6 without the skills they need.

Childcare is not a major concern so I would not focus on this if elected, but would try to decrease crime as this is a major concern in the community.

PART B Question 6 (continued)   MARKS

SOURCE 2

Selected Facts about Millwood

Millwood is a constituency for the UK Parliament in central Scotland. This part of Scotland used to rely on steelmaking as its main industry. There is now only one major employer, a call centre in the main town of Millwood. Last month it made 100 full time workers redundant. Parts of the area are amongst the most deprived in the UK and there are few job opportunities. Average life expectancy in the area is 77 compared to a UK average of 80.

Millwood Constituency is holding a by-election due to the death of the previous MP. Many people feel the area now needs an experienced representative.

There was a local meeting about crime levels last month in the town hall where 530 residents turned up to speak to the local community police officer about their concerns. Lynn Morrow, Chair of the Community Council said "Crime is clearly increasing. We are very worried about this issue. Our new MP needs to have a legal background".

Opinion Poll of 1000 Millwood Residents

	The elderly are well looked after in Millwood	Crime is a problem in Millwood	The UK Parliament needs more female MPs	A lack of childcare is a major problem locally
Strongly agree	12%	26%	21%	36%
Agree	23%	35%	33%	32%
Disagree	25%	30%	25%	22%
Strongly disagree	40%	9%	21%	10%

SOURCE 3

Millwood Statistics (%)

	Millwood	UK
Unemployed and seeking work	9	6
Claiming benefits	17·5	15·2
Full time employment	42	49
Women in work	34	45
Suffering long term ill health	15	18
Pupils completing S6 at school	56	53
Households with internet access	79	77

You must decide which option to recommend, **either** Nora Manson (**Option 1**) **or** John Donaldson (**Option 2**).

(i)   Using Sources 1, 2 and 3, **which option would you choose**?

(ii)   Give reasons to **support** your choice.

(iii) **Explain** why you did not choose the other option.

Your answer **must** be based on all three sources.   10

NOW GO TO SECTION 2 ON *PAGE TEN*

MARKS

SECTION 2 — SOCIAL ISSUES IN THE UNITED KINGDOM — 20 marks

Attempt ONE part, either

Part C — Social Inequality   on pages 10–13

OR

Part D — Crime and the Law   on pages 14–17

PART C — SOCIAL INEQUALITY

In your answers to Questions 7 and 8 you should give recent examples from the United Kingdom.

Question 7

> The UK Government tries to reduce social inequality.

Describe, **in detail**, **two** ways in which the UK Government tries to reduce social inequality.   4

Question 8

> There are many groups in the UK which experience inequality.

Explain, **in detail**, the reasons why one or more groups you have studied experiences inequality in the UK.   8

[Turn over for Question 9 on *Page twelve*

DO NOT WRITE ON THIS PAGE

PART C (continued)

Question 9

Study Sources 1, 2 and 3 and then answer the question which follows.

SOURCE 1

Poverty Factfile (2013 – 2014)

There are still 3·6 million children living in poverty in the United Kingdom. This means that a quarter (25%) of children in the UK currently live in poverty.

According to the UK Government, an average family needs to have £349 each week to meet their basic needs. The reality of living in poverty means that many families have only about £12 per day, per person to cover the basic cost of living. Children living in poverty often go without the items many children take for granted such as a bike or going on a school trip.

Poverty also has a negative impact on the health of a child with poor children experiencing more ill health than richer children. In addition, 24% of the poorest families cannot afford to keep their house warm compared to just 3% of wealthy families.

The UK Government is trying to reduce the problem of poverty. It recently set the ambitious targets that no more than 4% of children will be living in absolute poverty with a target of 12% for relative poverty by the year 2020. Absolute poverty is when someone cannot afford the basic necessities of life eg food, shelter. Relative poverty is in comparison to average incomes within a country.

Living in poverty can reduce a child's expectation of their own life and can often lead to a lifetime of poverty. Many people believe that it is the government's responsibility to help children improve their life chances and escape the cycle of poverty.

SOURCE 2

Selected Family Statistics

	Children Living in the Poorest Families	Children Living in the Richest Families
Average life expectancy at birth (years)	71	82
Childhood obesity rates	25%	18%
Average weekly family spending on food	£49	£70
Families who cannot afford a week's holiday per year	62%	6%

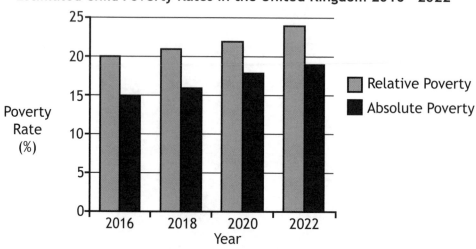

Estimated Child Poverty Rates in the United Kingdom 2016 – 2022

MARKS

PART C Question 9 (continued)

SOURCE 3

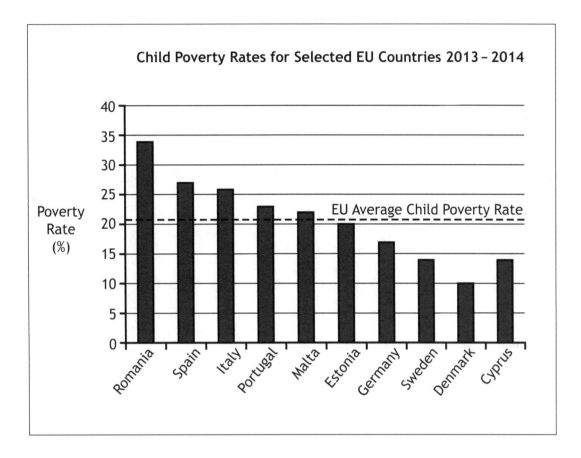

Child Poverty Rates for Selected EU Countries 2013 – 2014

Using Sources 1, 2 and 3, what **conclusions** can be drawn about the issue of child poverty.

You should reach a conclusion about **each** of the following.

- The impact of poverty on a child's life
- The UK Government's progress towards meeting its targets for 2020
- UK child poverty rates compared to other countries

Your conclusions **must** be supported by evidence from the sources. You should link information within and between the sources in support of your conclusions.

Your answer **must** be based on all three sources.

8

NOW GO TO SECTION 3 ON *PAGE EIGHTEEN*

MARKS

PART D — CRIME AND THE LAW

In your answers to Questions 10 and 11 you should give recent examples from the United Kingdom.

Question 10

> Scottish courts have the power to punish people.

Describe, **in detail**, **two** different ways that Scottish Courts can punish people.

4

Question 11

> There are many factors which cause crime in the UK.

Explain, **in detail**, the factors which cause crime in the UK.

8

[Turn over for Question 12 on *Page sixteen*

DO NOT WRITE ON THIS PAGE

PART D (continued)

Question 12

Study Sources 1, 2 and 3 below and then answer the question which follows.

SOURCE 1

Social Media and the Law

The law that has been used to prosecute people for sending inappropriate messages via social media is section 127 of the Communications Act 2003.

This states that a person is guilty of an offence if they send, post or forward a message online that is offensive or of an indecent, obscene or menacing character.

Social Media has become an important part of all areas of our daily lives. However, only one in five people (19%) read the terms and conditions of sites, and only one in ten know about social media laws, or have heard of the Communications Act 2003.

Communications sent via social media can be classed as criminal offences and companies now have more rules about the use of social media in their contracts and policies. A growing number of employers are now using social media sites to investigate people who have applied for a job. When surveyed, 63% of 16 to 18 year olds wrongly believed that this was against the law.

It is an offence to cause distress or threaten individuals online and those who embark on "trolling" can expect to be prosecuted by the police. Many people feel that they can behave differently online as they believe they are anonymous. However, more and more people are being prosecuted for their online activities and have received punishments from the courts.

Some police forces recognise that this is a very serious problem but they are extremely concerned that resources are being wasted — they estimate that two thirds of incidents reported to them are for petty online arguments.

SOURCE 2

Memo to Employees

G LENINCH COUNCIL

Dear Employees,

A recent University report suggests that the Scottish economy is losing millions of pounds because of workers using social media inappropriately during work time. Social media breaks are now costing us more than cigarette breaks!

Many of you will already be using social media in a variety of ways in your lives outside work. This memo will help you use social media responsibly at work.

We recognise the opportunities offered by social media and would like staff to use it to enhance the work of the Council.

However, you must respect the needs of the Council to protect its reputation.

If you use social media irresponsibly there is a risk that the Council will be damaged. We expect you to use social media responsibly and with care. If you do not do this you could be disciplined, face the sack or be prosecuted by the police. Sending inappropriate messages or taking social media breaks when you are supposed to be working will not be tolerated.

PART D Question 12 (continued)

SOURCE 3

Social Media Statistics

Opinion Poll

Question — Are you aware of the possible consequences of sending an offensive Tweet?

Yes	25%
No	75%

Social media – Complaints and prosecutions

	Complaints made to police about offensive posts on social media	Successful prosecutions
2010	2,347	60
2011	2,490	90
2012	2,563	107
2013	2,672	142
2014	2,703	240

Hours lost through social media breaks throughout the UK

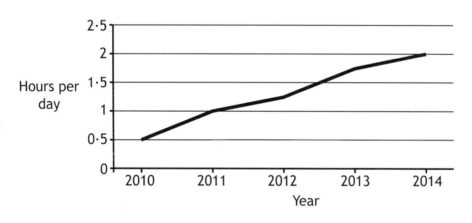

Using Sources 1, 2 and 3, what **conclusions** can be drawn about the law concerning social media.

You should reach a conclusion about each of the following:

- The level of public awareness of the law concerning social media
- Social media and the workplace
- Crime associated with social media.

Your conclusions must be supported by evidence from the sources. You should link information within and between the sources in support of your conclusions.

Your answer must be based on all three sources.

8

NOW GO TO SECTION 3 ON *PAGE EIGHTEEN*

MARK

SECTION 3 — INTERNATIONAL ISSUES — 20 marks

Attempt ONE part, either

Part E — World Powers   on pages 18–21

OR

Part F — World Issues   on pages 22–25

PART E — WORLD POWERS

In your answers to Questions 13 and 14 you should give recent examples from a world power you have studied.

Question 13

> World Powers can have an impact on other countries.

Describe, **in detail**, **two ways** the World Power you have studied has had an impact on other countries.

In your answer you should state the world power you have studied.   **6**

Question 14

> In all World Powers, some groups of people are poorly represented in government.

Explain, **in detail**, why some groups of people are poorly represented in the government of the world power you have studied.

In your answer you should state the world power you have studied.   **6**

[Turn over for Question 15 on *Page twenty*

DO NOT WRITE ON THIS PAGE

PART E (continued)

Question 15

Study Sources 1, 2 and 3 and then answer the question which follows.

Source 1

Gun Ownership in Selected G20 Countries

 USA – Guns : *ALLOWED*

According to the US Constitution all Americans can own a gun. A US Government report found that gun ownership increased from 192 million firearms in 1994 to 310 million firearms in 2009, but levels of crime fell sharply. Gun control campaigners argue that the easy availability of guns increases crime. The Brady Campaign to Prevent Gun Violence found that the US firearm homicide rate is 20 times higher than the combined rates of 22 countries with similar levels of wealth. A study from Harvard University said "there is no evidence which proves widespread gun ownership among the general population leads to higher incidents of murder."

FRANCE – Guns: *ALLOWED*   **JAPAN** – Guns: *BANNED*

Rules around gun ownership are strict eg you must see a doctor every year to get a certificate to prove you are physically and mentally able.

The weapons law begins by stating "No-one shall possess a firearm or firearms or a sword or swords", and very few exceptions are allowed.

BRAZIL – Guns: *ALLOWED*   **INDIA** – Guns: *BANNED*

In 2004, the number of gun-related injuries was 36,000. Despite this, in a 2005 referendum, 65% of the Brazilian population voted against banning the sale of guns and ammunition.

The law prevents the sale, manufacture, possession, import, export and transport of firearms and ammunition.

 RUSSIA – Guns: *BANNED*

Ownership of most types of guns is illegal for Russian civilians. Despite this, public shootings still happen. In November 2012, 30-year-old lawyer Dmitry Vinogradov walked into the Moscow offices of a medical company where he worked, and opened fire on his colleagues — murdering six and critically injuring one more. Right to Bear Arms, a Moscow based pressure group which represents gun owners, claimed "We have conducted studies which identify a clear pattern: the more a society is armed, the lower the level of criminal violence."

PART E Question 15 (continued)

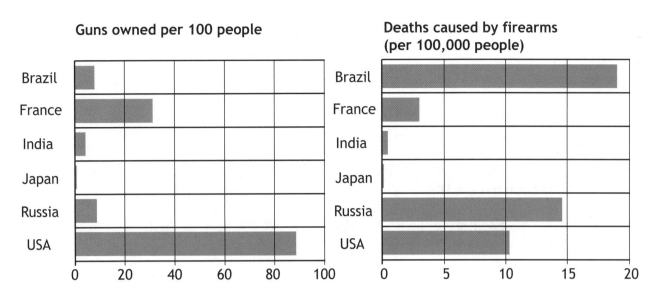

Source 2

More Guns = More Deaths?

SOURCE 3

Crime Statistics

Country	Murder Rate per 100,000	Violent Crime per 100,000	Robbery per 100,000
Brazil	27	504	110
France	1·65	201	100·8
India	1·5	162	1·6
Japan	0·4	98	4·0
Russia	10·2	584	90·3
USA	4·7	386	146·4

Using Sources 1, 2 and 3, explain why the view of **Kristen Nunez is selective in the use of facts.**

> Countries which allow gun ownership are safer places to live.
>
> View of Kristen Nunez

In your answer you must:

- give evidence from the sources that supports Kristen Nunez's view

and

- give evidence from the sources that opposes Kristen Nunez's view.

Your answer **must** be based on all three sources.

8

MARKS

PART F — WORLD ISSUES

In your answers to Questions 16 and 17 you should give recent examples from a world issue you have studied.

Question 16

Ordinary people are often affected by international issues and conflicts.

Describe, **in detail**, **two** ways ordinary people have been affected by an international issue **or** conflict you have studied.

In your answer you should state the world issue or conflict you have studied.

6

Question 17

International Organisations attempt to resolve issues and conflicts.

Selected International Organisations		
United Nations	NATO	European Union
Charities	NGOs	African Union

Select an International Organisation you have studied.

Explain, in detail, the reasons why it has succeeded **or** failed in resolving an international issue **or** conflict.

In your answer you should state the world issue or conflict you have studied.

6

[Turn over for Question 18 on *Page twenty-four*

DO NOT WRITE ON THIS PAGE

PART F (continued)

Question 18

Study Sources 1, 2 and 3 and then answer the question which follows.

Source 1

Illegal Drug Producers and Users

Drug producer: Afghanistan – Heroin and Marijuana

Afghanistan produces more opium than any other country in the world. Crops have dropped by 10% recently and the President recently stated that "Afghanistan is now a safer place to live." Almost all of the heroin used in Europe comes from Afghanistan's opium fields. In addition Afghanistan also supplies large amounts of marijuana to the world. Two aid workers travelling in Herat city were shot dead by an armed drug gang in July 2014.

Drug Producer: Peru – Cocaine and Heroin

Peru is the second largest producer of cocaine in the world. Until 1996, Peru was number one, but was then overtaken by Colombia.

Drug producer: Colombia – Cocaine

Colombia produces more cocaine than any other country in the world. They provide almost all of the cocaine consumed in the United States, as well as in other countries. Certain parts of the country are "no-go" areas for tourists and the police.

Drug user: The USA – Marijuana

Over 51% of all American adults have used marijuana at some stage in their lives. This is the highest figure in the world. Criminal gangs make billions of dollars and recently one gang member admitted to murdering forty enemies from other gangs. In a recent speech, President Obama stressed that the murder rate in the USA had halved in the last twenty years.

Drug user: Iran – Heroin

Iran has one of the highest rates of heroin use in the world. 2·3% of adults have used heroin in the last year.

Drug user: El Salvador – Cocaine

The small Central American country of El Salvador has a big issue with cocaine use. One in every forty people are regular users. Around 60 000 people are members of organised criminal gangs but the government has reduced the murder rate by 80% in recent years.

PART F Question 18 (continued)

Source 2

More Drugs = More Crime?

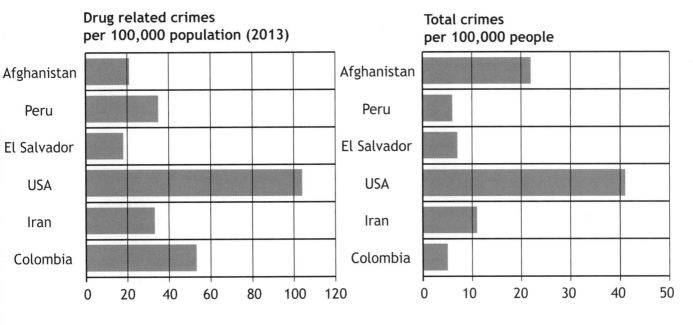

SOURCE 3

Crime Statistics

Country	Murder Rate per 100,000	Violent Kidnappings per 100,000	Serious Assaults per 100,000
Afghanistan	3·4	56	33
Peru	5·7	46	100
El Salvador	57·5	0·1	176
USA	4·7	17	874
Iran	3·9	4	44
Colombia	61·1	65	63

Using Sources 1, 2 and 3, explain why the view of **Ted King is selective in the use of facts.**

> Countries which produce illegal drugs are more dangerous places to live.
>
> View of Ted King

In your answer you must:

- give evidence from the sources that supports Ted King's view

and

- give evidence from the sources that opposes Ted King's view.

Your answer **must** be based on all three sources.   8

[END OF QUESTION PAPER]

MARKS

[BLANK PAGE]

DO NOT WRITE ON THIS PAGE

[BLANK PAGE]

DO NOT WRITE ON THIS PAGE

MARKS

[BLANK PAGE]

DO NOT WRITE ON THIS PAGE

SQA AND HODDER GIBSON NATIONAL 5 MODERN STUDIES 2015

Section 1

Part A

1. Reference to aspects of the following will be credited:
   - Make decisions about Education so affects availability of schools, etc.
   - Social housing affects the standards of housing in an area
   - Cleansing and recycling means refuse is taken away so areas are cleaner
   - Social work helps peoples' lives by supporting vulnerable groups
   - Community care affects the lives of elderly etc.
   - Decisions about Council Tax affect how much people have to pay

   Below is a model paragraph answer – 3 marks awarded.

   Local councils affect the lives of Scottish people in many ways. One way is through the collection of refuse or waste. In some local authorities there are many different collections. This may be to try and increase recycling or "greener" ways of reusing our waste. An example would be North Lanarkshire who have collections for Garden waste, collections for paper and other recyclables, "food only" waste bins as well as general waste. **4**

2. Reference to aspects of the following will be credited:

   Happy with the way AMS has worked
   - Fairer/more proportional so voters' choices more likely to be reflected in Parliament
   - Each voter has two votes so able to split vote – greater choice
   - More representatives to choose from ie constituency and 7 regional MSPs
   - Has resulted in 8 years of coalition government with reasonable stability as well as produced one minority and one majority government – with a reasonable degree of success (so far)

   Unhappy with the way AMS has worked
   - Complex voting system may cause confusion as in 2007 with many "lost" or "wasted" votes
   - Two types of MSP elected with some confusion over roles
   - Not completely proportional – still over-represents larger parties ie Labour and SNP while under-representing smaller parties

   Below is a model paragraph answer – 4 marks awarded.

   One way people are happy with the Additional Member System is the greater representation of smaller parties. In AMS, voters have two votes, one for an individual constituency MSP like Fiona McLeod with the 2nd vote being for a party. From this Regional List MSPs such as Annabel Goldie are created using the d'Hont formula which gives smaller parties greater representation. For example, in every election since 1999 the Green Party has had representation in the parliament. **8**

3. You are required to evaluate a limited range of sources detecting and explaining instances of exaggeration and/or selective use of facts, giving developed answers.

To achieve full marks you must show evidence that has been selected as it supports the view and show evidence that has not been selected, as it does not support the view.

An answer which deals with only one side of your explanation will be awarded a maximum of 6 marks.

Below is a model answer – awarded full marks 8/8.

Gillian Duffy is not being selective when she says "new tax-raising powers for the Scottish Parliament would be good for Scotland" as Source 1 states that this would make the Scottish Parliament more accountable as voters could choose the party which had the tax and spending policies they supported. Again Source 1 states that this proposal is the next step to increase the powers of the devolved Parliament now that it has been established for over 20 years. These views are supported in Source 3 which shows that the Scottish public overwhelmingly trust the Scottish Government more than the UK Government – 60% to only 24 % – so it would be good for Scotland.

Gillian Duffy is being selective as Source 1 states that this change could lead to higher taxes in Scotland compared to England, which could be bad and it could reduce the influence of the UK Government. In source 2 we see that the public think that the UK Government has the most influence over the way Scotland is run and this is the way it should be as in Source 1 the Scottish Government only has devolved powers.

She is also being selective as Source 1 states that new tax powers would give the UK Government an excuse to reduce the funding to the Scottish Government and Parliament and this could lead to less spending on health and education and this could make the Scottish Government less popular and reduce trust. This could be problem as in Source 3 we see that trust in the Scottish Parliament has declined from 70% in 2007 to 60% in 2009. **8**

Part B

1. Reference to aspects of the following will be credited:
   - Discusses laws in depth as they have time
   - Brings experience to discussions
   - Can delay legislation
   - May be able to force government to rethink legislation or policy
   - Can be used to "elevate" former senior MPs etc.
   - Can bring ministers into the Government

   Below is a model paragraph answer – 3 marks awarded.

   One way in which the Lords can play a part in decision making is that it can amend most bills if the majority of peers have issues with some of the details. For example, the coalition government's Health and Social Care Bill experienced a number of amendments as it passed through the Lords including setting up patient councils in England & Wales to monitor health care. **4**

2. Reference to aspects of the following will be credited:

   Positive
   - Media – provide information for voters about political issues so makes them more informed as voters
   - Media – exposes wrongdoing on the part of politicians and parties and so holds them to account

- Media – broadcast media such as TV and Radio need to be neutral and objective
- Trade Unions – provide an influential body to promote workers' rights and conditions
- Trade Unions – their peaceful protests help promote democracy
- Trade Unions – their relationship with the Labour party provides representation for all sections of society
- Pressure Groups – help provide influence for minority groups
- Pressure Groups – provide information for voters about political issues
- Pressure Groups – keep people involved in politics due to popularity

Negative
- Media – newspapers concentrate on scandal and create a cynical attitude amongst voters leading to decline in interest in politics and voting
- Media – some newspapers are not serious and trivialise and over simplify matters which leaves voters less well informed
- Media – some newspapers are very biased and do not give voters a balanced view of issues
- Trade Unions – they can hold the Government to ransom through the threat of strike
- Trade Unions – some feel their relationship with the Labour party has too much influence on decision-making
- Trade Unions – can cause disruption for many people – BA strikes
- Pressure Groups – sometimes give a minority too much influence
- Pressure Groups – occasionally protests can turn violent/disruptive – eg 2011 student riots
- Pressure Groups – some PGs are very large and through lobbying can have too much influence over government policy

Below is a model paragraph answer – 4 marks awarded.

> Some people think that the media plays a positive role in politics as it gives political parties an opportunity to inform voters about party policies. During election time, there are party political broadcasts on the TV. The time that is given to these broadcasts are based on the balance of power in parliament, therefore, they are fair. These party political broadcasts are usually on TV at peak times thus reaching as wide an audience as possible. Watching these broadcasts allow voters to use their vote in an informed way. **8**

3. You are required to evaluate a limited range of sources, detecting and explaining instances of exaggeration and/or selective use of facts, giving developed arguments.

To achieve full marks you must show evidence that has been selected as it supports the view and show evidence that has not been selected, as it does not support the view.

An answer that deals with only one side of the explanation, will only be awarded a maximum of 6 marks.

Below is a model answer – awarded full marks 8/8.

> Adam Stewart is being selective when he says "The party leaders' debates in the 2010 election had little impact on the election campaign" as according to Source 1, millions of viewers watched the debates and turnout increased by 4% compared with 2005. This is further supported by Source 3 which shows viewing figures of 9.4m, 4.1m and 8.4m for the three leaders' debates.
>
> Adam Stewart is also being selective as according to Source 1 it was the first time in the UK televised

leaders' debates were held and in source 2 it states that a massive 69% of people felt it was a positive change in the election.

> However, Adam Stewart is not being selective when he says "The party leaders' debates in the 2010 election had little impact on the election campaign" as according to Source 1 Conservatives were predicted to win and they were the largest party after the election. Also he is not being selective as according to Source 2 some people believed the debates would have little impact on the result as most people have made up their minds, before the election, about who they will vote for. In fact, according to Source 2, a huge 68% felt that the debates would make no difference. **8**

Section 2

Part C

1. Reference to aspects of the following will be credited:

Scottish Government
- Smoking ban
- Other actions to reduce smoking, eg age of purchase, display of cigarettes
- Measures to reduce alcohol consumption – minimum pricing
- Role of NHS Scotland in improving health – advertising, eg 5-a-day
- NHS Health Scotland
- Health Promoting Schools

Local Councils
- Free access to leisure facilities for school children
- Healthy eating initiatives in schools
- Free school meals P1–3

Below is a model paragraph answer – 3 marks awarded.

> The Scottish Government has introduced a number of laws to improve health such as the smoking ban. The smoking ban was introduced in 2006 and banned smoking in public places such as bars and restaurants. This has reduced the amount of people smoking and the amount of people affected by passive smoking – due to this, cancer rates have fallen. **4**

2. Reference to aspects of the following will be credited:
- Low pay leading to low living standards
- Unemployment leading to reliance on benefits
- Lone parents/family structure
- Alcohol/drugs addiction – leading to unemployment
- Lack of skills/qualifications – confined to low-paid, insecure jobs
- Lack of suitable/well-paid employment because of decline of industry in certain areas

Below is a model paragraph answer – 4 marks awarded.

> A reason people live in poverty is due to unemployment. The current recession in the UK has led to high levels of unemployment and many people find themselves out of work. Living on benefits does not provide adequate income and a person who has been unemployed for a long period will struggle to make ends meet and suffer from social exclusion. Long-term unemployment is a major concern for the UK Government and a main reason for people finding themselves stuck in the poverty trap. **6**

3. You must use a limited range of sources by selecting evidence from them in order to make and justify a decision/recommendation.

You will be awarded up to three marks for a justification depending on relevance and development of the evidence.

You will be highly credited if you make justifications which show interaction between the sources.

For full marks, you must justify your decision/recommendation and explain why you have rejected the other option. Answers, which deal with only one decision, will be awarded a maximum of eight marks.

Across the whole answer you must use all 3 sources to achieve full marks.

Below is a model answer – awarded full marks 10/10.

> In my role as government advisor I have decided to recommend Option 1 that the Government should continue with the system of Working Tax Credits (WTC).
>
> The first reason to back my recommendation is found in Source 1 where it states that "over half a million children have been lifted out of poverty as more people on low or moderate incomes have been helped." This benefit is highlighted in Source 2 where figures show that child poverty figures have declined. In 2001 3 million children lived in poverty and by 2010 this figure was 2.5 million. The Government Spokesperson in Source 3 underlines this reason stating "the tax credit system has helped many families to get out of poverty." If WTCs are reducing poverty they should be continued.
>
> Another reason to back Option 1 is found in Source 1 where it states "Working Tax Credit allows families to get back up to 80% of the cost of childcare allowing adults to go back to work." This links in with Source 3 where the Government Spokesperson states that "Working Tax Credits encourage people to work and also gives help with childcare costs." In allowing people to get back to work in this way WTCs should undoubtedly continue.
>
> Lastly, Source 3 states "the problem faced by many was that if they came off benefits and went into low paid jobs, they were worse off." Working Tax Credits have stopped this as Source 1 points out "Working Tax Credits have helped people to beat the poverty trap – it makes sure a person's income is better in work than out of work and living on benefits."
>
> The reason I didn't choose Option 2 is, although Source 1 states "there have been problems with overpayments being made", the Government Spokesperson in Source 3 states "despite problems in overpayments in the first few years, many of these difficulties have been sorted." **10**

Part D

1. Reference to aspects of the following will be credited:
   - Vandalism
   - Shoplifting
   - Breach of the peace
   - Under-age drinking – related crimes
   - Drug offences
   - Graffiti
   - Car theft
   - Hanging around the streets/causing a disturbance

   Below is a model paragraph answer – 3 marks awarded.

   > If young people do commit crimes they tend to be crimes associated with anti-social behaviour. Young people may drink alcohol and then be more likely to cause breach of the peace. This could include hanging about housing estates or shops in gangs and partaking in rowdy behaviour. **4**

2. Reference to aspects of the following will be credited:

   Community Policing
   - In residential areas where the police can get to know the residents and local young people
   - People feel safer in their communities knowing there are police on the beat
   - Young people may respond to community initiatives and be less likely to vandalise/get involved in anti-social behaviour
   - People may not want CCTV cameras in their local communities

   CCTV Cameras
   - In shopping centres/High Streets where shoplifting and pick-pocketing is a problem
   - In areas where recording the entrances and exits to facilities will help to identify those who have committed crimes
   - Too expensive to police such large areas
   - A police presence may not be desirable

   Below is a model paragraph answer – 4 marks awarded.

   > People believe community policing is effective as it allows the police to get to know local residents and young people in a certain area and hopefully build relationships that will reduce crime. However, some people argue CCTV is an effective way of tackling crime. In areas such as city centres, CCTV cameras can monitor large areas where the police may not be able to patrol at all times. This can be particularly useful at busy weekend periods such as pub/club closing times. **6**

3. You must use a limited range of sources by selecting evidence from them in order to make and justify a decision/recommendation.

   You will be awarded up to three marks for a justification depending on relevance and development of the evidence.

   You will be highly credited if you make justifications which show interaction between the sources.

   For full marks, you must justify your decision/recommendation and explain why you have rejected the other option. Answers, which deal with only one decision, will be awarded a maximum of eight marks.

   Across the whole answer you must use all 3 sources to achieve full marks.

   Below is a model answer – awarded full marks 10/10.

   > In my role as government advisor I have decided to recommend Option 1 that the DNA database should contain profiles of the whole population.
   >
   > Source 1 highlights the first reason for my recommendation as it states "most people would approve of a new law requiring all adults to give a sample of their DNA to help with prevention and detection of crime." This is backed up in Source 2 where it shows that 66% of people polled in an opinion survey agreed that there should be a new law requiring everyone over 18 to give a sample of DNA.
   >
   > Another reason to back my recommendation is in Source 1 where it states "ethnic minorities are more likely, at present, to be on the database than white people." This is backed up in Source 2 where figures show that 37% of blacks and 13% of Asians are on the DNA database compared to only 9% of whites. This links with Source 3 where the Police Spokesperson states that "having everyone on the database means there will be no discrimination against ethnic minorities." The race issue

regarding the database would be solved if everyone gave their DNA.

Another reason to back Option 1 is found in Source 3 where the Police Spokesperson states "DNA evidence… will help the police convict the right person in the most serious of crimes." This is backed up in Source 1 which states "if the whole population had their DNA profiles on the database, this would help in the investigation and prosecution of crime." In the opinion poll in Source 2 65% of people stated that DNA evidence was more important than any other type of evidence. DNA would ultimately help in convicting guilty people.

I did not choose Option 2 as, although the Civil Rights Spokesperson states "the DNA database should be kept for profiles of convicted criminals only", Source 1 states "money and time would be saved if everyone's DNA profile was taken only once."   10

Section 3

Part E

1. Clear reference to specific political institutions of chosen G20 country. Reference to aspects of the following will be credited:
   - Different levels of government
   - Democratic structures
   - Voting in elections at various levels
   - Opportunities for political participation
   - Specific USA reference to aspects of Executive, Legislature and Judiciary and separation of powers

   Below is a model paragraph answer – 3 marks awarded.

   The country I have studied is the USA.

   The American Constitution outlines the powers of the different institutions. The President is also elected every four years and they are in charge of the Executive. The President proposes laws which are implemented by Congress and judged legal by the Supreme Court.   6

2. Reference to aspects of the following will be credited:
   - Educational inequality issues in your selected country
   - Any issues relating to health and health-care inequalities within your selected country
   - Issues relating to law and order within your selected country
   - Differences in housing between different groups in your selected country

   Below is a model paragraph answer – 4 marks allocated.

   In the USA health inequalities continue to be a problem. In the USA you have to buy private medical insurance from a company such as BlueCross. This means that many people in poverty do not have any medical insurance and so receive only very basic medical care. It is estimated that up to 40 million Americans do not have adequate medical cover. This has led to huge inequalities in some parts of the USA which at times can be related to race with Blacks and Hispanics being more likely to suffer from poverty and not be covered by private medical insurance.   6

3. You are required to use the sources provided to draw valid conclusions, with supporting evidence

   You should draw conclusions using the headings/bullet points in the question.

   An answer which merely repeats the source material without making judgements or conclusions will be awarded zero marks.

For full marks three developed conclusions must be given.

You should link information within and between sources in support of your conclusion.

The conclusion can be placed either at the beginning or at the end after the evidence.

Below is a model answer – awarded full marks 8/8.

Ethnic composition in different parts of the country

The conclusion is by far that Han is the largest ethnic group in the G20 country.

According to Source 1, "the largest ethnic group, by far, is the Han". This is supported by Source 3 which shows that 5 out of the 6 regions are dominated by Han. Only Tibet is not dominated by Han.

The link between income and education

The conclusion is that those on lower income are more likely to be unable to read or write.

According to Source 1 there are big differences in levels of income within different parts of the country, with coastal regions having considerably more wealth. Income differences are important because they will have an effect upon education. This is supported by Source 2 which shows that the three inland areas which are poorest have rates that range from 19.7% to 54.9%, whereas in richer coastal areas the figure ranges from 4.6% to 7.6%.

Health in urban and rural areas

The conclusion is that rural areas have worse health than urban areas.

According to Source 1 there are big differences in health and education between rural and urban areas. The source goes on to explain that this is because "rural areas are poorer and so too are health facilities". Source 2 further emphasises this by showing that in the three rural areas life expectancy is substantially lower than in the three urban areas. In fact, in the most rural area Tibet, life expectancy is 64 years old contrasting with the most urban area Shanghai in which life expectancy is 78.   8

Part F

1. Reference to aspects of the following will be credited:

   Issue – Terrorism
   - Nationalism – Palestine/Israel
   - Political unrest – Syria
   - Religious Extremism – Afghanistan/Taliban/Al Qaeda
   - Discrimination
   - Poverty

   Below is a model paragraph answer – 3 marks awarded.

   There are various causes of terrorism. Firstly, a group may resort to terrorist acts to try to achieve a nationalist goal. This means they believe their region or country should have independence from another country. A group of people may not believe national independence is possible through the ballot box and in turn decide to turn to terrorist methods to achieve their aims.   6

2. Reference to aspects of the following will be credited:

Issue – Terrorism

- NATO- Difficulties in Afghanistan and Iraq, residence from Taliban and other extremist organisations
- European Union – sharing of intelligence, human rights
- United Nations – Differing views of member countries on what constitutes terrorism (USA/Russia on Syria, views on Palestine/Israel etc). Veto of Security Council in dealing with countries that facilitate terrorist activity

Below is a model paragraph answer – 4 marks awarded.

The European Union (EU) has responded to terrorism by increasing cooperation between member states. However, many EU nations have encountered difficulties in dealing with suspected terrorists from other countries as they have not been able to deport them back to their country of origin. Often this is associated with a person's human rights and EU countries have to be careful not to prevent anyone from receiving their human rights as outlined by the UN.   6

3. You are required to use the sources provided to draw valid conclusions, with supporting evidence

You should draw conclusions using the headings/bullet points in the question.

An answer which merely repeats the source material without making judgements or conclusions will be awarded zero marks.

For full marks three developed conclusions must be given.

You should link information within and between sources in support of your conclusions.

The conclusion can be placed either at the beginning or at the end after the evidence.

Below is a model answer – awarded full marks 8/8.

The success of the G8 in meeting Promise 1: To improve Health Care

The conclusion is that G8 countries have been very successful in meeting Promise 1.

Using Source 1, we see that Promise 1 is to improve health and Source 1 also shows that the % of people in Rwanda with HIV decreased from 7.0 in 1996 to 2.8 in 2009. Source 3 provided further evidence of improved health with infant mortality rates declining and life expectancy rising in all three countries. In Malawi, infant mortality rates have declined from 122 in 1996 to 65 in 2009 and in Ethiopia life expectancy has increased from 49 to 56.

The success of the G8 in meeting Promise 2

The conclusion is that that the G8 countries have not been successful at all in meeting Promise 2.

Using Source 1, we see that Promise 2 is to more than double total ODA given to all less developed countries by 2010 and Source 1 also shows that Canada almost reached Promise 2 with its ODA spend increasing from $2.6 billion in 2004 to $5.1 billion in 2010. In Source 2 the figure for the UK went from $7.9 billion to $13.8 billion. Again, this has not more than doubled. This was the same for the other G8 countries in the table, all failed to more than double their ODA contribution.

The G8 country most committed to meeting the UN aid recommendation

The conclusion is that the UK is the G8 country most committed to meeting the UN aid recommendation.

In Source 1 it states that the UN recommendation is 0.7% of a country's GNI be set aside as ODA. Source 2 shows that in 2010 the country giving the highest % of GNI as ODA was the UK at 0.56%. This is below the UN recommendation but it does make the UK the most committed G8 country. Italy was the less committed with its % of GNI remaining the same in 2005 and 2010 at 0.15%. All other countries increased their % of GNI but none reached the figure of 0.7%.   8

NATIONAL 5 MODERN STUDIES MODEL PAPER 2

Section 1

Part A

1. Reference to aspects of the following will be credited:
   - Health and social work
   - Education and training
   - Local Government and housing
   - Justice and police
   - Agriculture, forestry and fisheries
   - The environment
   - Tourism, sport and heritage
   - Economic development and internal transport

   Below is a model paragraph answer – 3 marks awarded.

   > One devolved matter in which the Scottish government can make decisions is health care. All health care decisions are made in Scotland for Scotland with decisions about new hospitals and care for the elderly devolved. An example is the Government's decisions to ban the display of cigarettes in large shops to try and stop people being attracted to smoking. **4**

2. Reference to aspects of the following will be credited:
   - Grants from Scottish Government (revenue and capital)
   - Council tax
   - Non-domestic rates
   - Charges for council provided services, including rent
   - Sales
   - PPP projects or similar

   Below is a model paragraph answer – 4 marks awarded.

   > Local Authorities can raise funds in a number of ways. Their main income is from council tax which is charged to every household. This tax is used to pay for huge variety of services. For example, Local Authorities provide state education and money raised from council taxes will help pay for local schools and nurseries. Council tax varies depending on which area you stay in and the number of rooms within the house. **6**

3. You are required to evaluate a limited range of sources, in order to make and justify a decision/recommendation.

   You must also explain why you have rejected the other option.

   In order to achieve full marks you must say why you did not choose the other option. If your answer deals with only one option it will be awarded a maximum of 8 marks.

   Below is a model answer – awarded full marks 10/10.

   #### For Ian MacKay

   > The candidate I would choose would be Ian MacKay. One reason why I chose him is that Ian supports the golf development because he says that a lot of jobs will be provided for the local area. This is true as Source 2 clearly states that the Inverdon Dunes Golf Development will create 5,000 temporary and 1,250 permanent jobs. This will be particularly good for Inverdon as Source 1 shows that unemployment in Inverdon is running at 4.2% which is above the Scottish average of 4%. The possibility of new jobs would, therefore, be most welcome.
   >
   > Another reason why I have chosen Ian is his concern about the number of migrant workers moving to the area, and most local people agree. This is supported by the Public Opinion Survey in Source 3 which shows that 55% think that Inverdon does not need more migrant workers. According to the Source 2 the jobs that will be created will be skilled or highly skilled and according to Source 1 these will not be attractive to migrant workers.
   >
   > Lastly, Ian also says that, although some wildlife tourists will be lost, many more golf tourists will be attracted. This is supported by Source 2 with the information that 25,000 wildlife tourists visit the area at the moment. However, as many as 100,000 golf tourists could be attracted by the new development.
   >
   > One reason I did not chose Sally Anderson is that she states that the vast majority of the public agree with her view and do not support the development and don't think the area needs a boost to local businesses. However, Source 3 shows that 65%, which is the majority, say "Yes" to supporting the golf development. This is further backed up by Source 1, which states that the area needs a boost to the local economy. **10**

Part B

1. Reference to aspects of the following will be credited:

   Help in election campaign by
   - Canvassing in person
   - Telephone canvassing
   - Delivery of election materials
   - Talking to voters to persuade them to support candidate
   - Administrative work in candidate's office
   - Giving lifts to voters on day of election
   - Taking part in publicity events

   National campaign has major impact on local campaigns
   - Setting agenda
   - National media campaigns

   Below is a model paragraph answer – 3 marks awarded.

   > Political parties campaign to get their candidates elected by producing a large number and variety of election materials. These take the form of leaflets, placards and posters. Political parties will recruit volunteers to distribute these materials, usually in town or city centres. Quite often political parties will also go door-to-door to try to convince the public to vote for their candidate – this is known as canvassing. **4**

2. Reference to aspects of the following will be credited:

   Changes
   - Wish to see all or some of House of Lords elected as it is undemocratic at present
   - Wish to see wider range of members as unrepresentative at moment
   - Wish to see end to patronage as PM/governing party can appoint supporters
   - Wish to see more powers as able to check power of Commons, eg power of veto rather than delay only, no power over money bills
   - Wish to see more modern working practices as many are outdated
   - Wish to see introduction of PR system of voting

   Below is a model paragraph answer – 4 marks awarded.

   > Some people want changes made to the House of Lords as they see it as being undemocratic. At the moment peers are unelected as honours are given out by the Prime Minister for life. Many want there to be elections for some or all peers. They believe that the Lords will then become more accountable and will therefore

make decisions with the public interest in mind rather than another agenda. The Liberal Democrats have long been supporters of reform, however, despite several movements to reform the Upper Chamber, it has remained largely unchanged since the last reforms in 1999.   **6**

3. You are required to evaluate a limited range of sources, in order to make and justify a decision/recommendation.

   You must also explain why you have rejected the other option.

   In order to achieve full marks you must say why you did not choose the other option. If your answer deals with only one option it will be awarded a maximum of 8 marks.

   Below is a mode answer – awarded full marks 10/10.

   ### For Kirsty Reid

   The candidate I would chose is Kirsty Reid as she supports the quarry because it will provide jobs to stop the decline of the local economy. This is backed up by the background information which shows that 150 new jobs will be created in the quarry. This is supported by Source 2 which shows that jobs are the issue that is seen as very important – 52%.

   Also, according to Source 1 there are a number of transport problems in the constituency, including high petrol prices and poor public transport. In Source 3 Kirsty Reid says that she will make improving transport links a priority to attract more business to the area. This will help with a number of issues in Gleninch such as the huge unemployment rate which is 13% above the Scottish average.

   She also states that these jobs are needed to keep young people in the area. This is backed up by Source 1 which states that many young people in the area move away to big cities.

   The reason I did not chose Robbie MacKay is because he opposes the new quarry because according to him the local party are more concerned about the environment than jobs. However, this is not true. The survey shows that 52% think that jobs are very important, compared to only 30% for the environment. Also according to Source 1 tourism is becoming less important to the local economy, with those employed in hotels, bed and breakfast accommodation and restaurants on the decline.   **10**

Section 2

Part C

1. Credit reference to aspects of the following:
   - Child Benefit – helps families with children under the age of 16
   - Housing Benefit – helps those on a low income to pay their rent
   - Jobseekers Allowance – helps those who are looking for a job
   - State Pension – helps those who have retired
   - Tax Credits – supports families on a low income
   - Educational Maintenance Allowance (EMA)
   - Cold Weather Payments
   - Employment and Support Allowance
   - Income Support
   - Incapacity Benefits

   Below is a model paragraph answer – 3 marks awarded.

   The Government provides a "safety net" for the population should a person fall on hard times and require support – this is called the Welfare State. One way the Government helps people is through various forms of financial support. Firstly, if a person loses their job the Government will help them until they find another. This unemployed benefit is called Job Seekers Allowance, which usually amounts to around £57 per week.   **6**

2. Reference to aspects of the following will be credited:
   - Lifestyle factors – eg the effects of smoking, drink/alcohol abuse, lack of exercise
   - Social and economic disadvantages – eg poor diet, effects of poverty
   - Geography and environment – eg poor quality housing, limited access to local amenities, high levels of crime
   - Gender – women live longer than men but are more likely to suffer poor health
   - Race – high incidence of heart attacks, strokes, depression etc. Also more likely to be poor and therefore to suffer ill health due to this

   Below is a model paragraph answer – 4 marks awarded.

   Health inequalities continue to exist in the UK because many people continue to make poor lifestyle choices. Choosing to smoke, excessively drink alcohol and eat a fatty diet can lead to complex health issues such as diabetes, heart attacks and strokes. Life expectancy among people who make poor lifestyle choices and don't exercise is significantly lower than those who choose to lead a healthy life. Across Glasgow there are vast life expectancy differences with poorer people tending to make worse lifestyle choices than those better off.   **6**

3. You are required to use the sources provided to draw valid conclusions, with supporting evidence.

   You should draw conclusions using the headings/bullet points in the question.

   An answer which merely repeats the source material without making judgements or conclusions will be awarded zero marks.

   For full marks three developed conclusions must be given.

   You should link information within and between sources in support of your conclusions.

   The conclusion can be placed either at the beginning or at the end after the evidence.

   Below is a model answer – awarded full marks 8/8.

   ### Changes in marriage and divorce in Britain

   The first conclusion is that the rate of marriages has decreased and the rate of divorces has increased.

   Source 1 shows that the rate of marriages has fallen by around 50% from 1970 to 2005. The source also shows that the rate of divorces has increased from around 75,000 per year in 1970 to 180,000 in 2005. Source 3 also states "from 1970 to 2005 there has been a large drop in marriages in general but not in divorces."

   ### The link between changes in marriages and changes in the "traditional" family

   Another conclusion is that as the percentage of marriages fell, the percentage of the "traditional" family fell also.

   Source 2 states that "the 'traditional' family has always been seen as a couple with dependent children". The % of the "traditional" family has fallen from 52% of households in 1971 to 35% in 2009. Source 1 highlights that in the same time period, between 1970 and 2005, marriages have decreased by more than 50%.

The main difference between ethnic minority families and white families

My final conclusion is that Whites have the lowest percentage of married couples and the highest percentage of lone parent families compared to all other ethnic groups.

Source 3 backs this up, stating that Whites only have a married couple's percentage of 62% where as the table shows Indians at a massive 83% and Bangladeshi, Chinese and Pakistani all ahead of Whites. Indians also have the lowest rate of lone parent families at 12% compared to Whites at 25%. This links in with Source 2 where it states "white people in Britain have the lowest percentage of married couples." **8**

Part D

1. Reference to aspects of the following will be credited:

District Court/Justice of the Peace Court
- The longest prison sentence which can be imposed is generally 60 days
- The maximum fine of up to £2500
- Minor offences

Sheriff Court
- Summary procedure – a sheriff may impose prison sentences of up to 3 months, in some cases up to 12 months. Fines up to £5000. No jury present – less serious cases
- Solemn procedure – unlimited financial penalties – can refer to the High Court, also has a range of non-custodial options such as community service and probation. Jury present – serious cases

High Court (of Justiciary)
- Judge presides
- Most serious crimes such as rape, assault and murder
- Jury of 15
- Custodial and non-custodial sentencing options

Court of Session
- Civil cases

Below is a model paragraph answer – 3 marks awarded.

Within the adult court system in Scotland there are various courts that deal with a range of crimes and offences. Firstly, the Justice of the Peace Courts in Scotland (formerly known as District Courts) deal with minor offences such as breach of the peace and driving offences. In these courts there is no jury or judge and sentencing powers are limited to a max fine of £2500 and 60 days in prison. **6**

2. Reference to aspects of the following will be credited:
- Overcrowding and other poor conditions against prisoners' human rights and does not encourage rehabilitation
- Used too frequently – young people into prison system too early
- Lack of staff and funding to run rehabilitation programmes
- High level of recidivism
- Contributes to breakup of families
- Prison is too lenient – not seen as a deterrent
- Too many early releases – insufficient note taken of views and feelings of victims and their families
- High cost of prison system – not effective use of resources

Below is a model paragraph answer – 4 marks awarded.

Critics argue that prisons cost too much to run. The cost of putting someone in prison for a year is around £40,000, therefore, the prison system in Scotland is a massive burden on the tax payer. Critics argue the focus should be put on rehabilitating criminals, especially those who are repeat offenders. The costs of alternative sentences such as community service are much lower than sending someone to prison, and such a sentence will teach a criminal about the consequences of their actions. **6**

3. You are required to use the sources provided to draw valid conclusions, with supporting evidence.

You should draw conclusions using the headings/bullet points in the question.

An answer which merely repeats the source material without making judgements or conclusions will be awarded zero marks.

For full marks three developed conclusions must be given.

You should link information within and between sources in support of your conclusions.

The conclusion can be placed either at the beginning or at the end after the evidence.

Below is a model answer – awarded full marks 8/8.

The rate of murders with knives

My first conclusion is that the rate of murders with knives is decreasing.

This is supported by evidence from Source 2 which shows that in 2003/2004 there were 70 murders involving knives in Scotland and as the years have progressed this has decreased to a low of 49 in 2007/2008. This links in with Source 1 which states "the threat of a custodial sentence may work as the number of murders with knives has dropped since 2003/2004."

The reasons young people carry knives

The conclusion is that young people carry knives for a variety of reasons.

Source 1 tells us that "some young people carry a knife for their own personal safety when they go out." However, Source 3 states "many youths have stated that carrying a knife is part of being in a gang and they have to be seen to be armed – peer pressure is a key factor."

The views on methods to reduce knife crime

My conclusion is that most people believe a jail sentence will reduce knife crime.

This is supported by Source 2 where it shows that in a public opinion survey 67% of people believed an automatic jail sentence reduces knife crime and only 29% think community service or a fine (4%) was the correct method. This links with Source 1 which states "Many members of the public believe that people who carry knives should automatically be sent to jail which would reduce crime – very few people think a fine would work." Lastly my conclusion is backed up by Source 3, which states "young people have admitted that a jail sentence would make them think twice about carrying a knife." **8**

Section 3

Part E

1. Credit will be given to answers which describe government responses to social inequalities, economic inequalities or a combination of the two.

   Reference to aspects of the following will be credited:
   - Educational issues in your selected country
   - Any issues relating to health care and inequalities within your selected country
   - Issues relating to law and order within your selected country
   - Differences in housing between different groups in your selected country
   - Wealth, employment and living standards inequalities in your selected country

   Below is a model paragraph answer – 3 marks awarded.

   The country I have studied is South Africa.

   Within education the South African Government has responded to the poor educational attainment of many of its country's young people by increasing spending on education – in 2012 it invested 21% of the entire spending on education. Students in poorer schools do not need to pay school fees. New schools have also been built and in the Western Cape only 4% of schools have no electricity.

   6

2. Reference to aspects of the following will be credited:
   - Access to elections within your selected country
   - Level of choice and competition between political parties/candidates within your selected country
   - The extent to which freedom of speech, religion, media is allowed, ie protest, Internet within your selected country
   - Political integrity and no corruption within your selected country

   Below is a model paragraph answer – 4 marks awarded.

   The country I have studied is South Africa.

   Within South Africa opposition parties and concerned citizens such as Desmond Tutu are worried by government attempts to limit the freedom of the press and reduce people's political rights. The South African Broadcasting Corporation (SABC) is regarded as the mouthpiece of the ANC and at election time it favours the ANC. The press have until now been able to publish corruption and criminal actions by ANC leaders. However the ANC Government intend to pass a law, which makes it a crime to report on the activities of government politicians.

   6

3. You are required to evaluate a limited range of sources, detecting and explaining instances of exaggeration and/or selective use of facts, giving developed arguments.

   To achieve full marks you must show evidence that has been selected as it supports the view and show evidence that has not been selected, as it does not support the view.

   An answer that deals with only one side of the explanation, or does not use evidence from all sources will only be awarded a maximum of 6 marks.

   Below is a model answer – awarded full marks 8/8.

   Brad Simpson is not being selective in the use of facts when he says "The President... remains popular amongst his own party". This is because according to Source 1 the President's popularity has remained steadily between 80–90% of his own part between April 2009 – August 2010. This backed up in Source 3 when it says that support from the President's own political party has changed little.

   However, he is being selective when he says "The President remains popular, especially on the main issue for all ethnic groups". This statement is incorrect because on the issues of the Economy and Terrorism, the President did have the support of the majority of White, Black and Hispanic Americans. However, on the issue of health, the President did not have the support of the majority of White Americans as only 40% were in favour of his reforms. Also according to Source 1 the opposition party, which has a key demographic of Asians, has seen a fall in support for the President from 40% to below 20%.

   Also, he is not being selective as Source 2 shows that in 8 of the 9 states more people agree with the view that he is doing a good job. However while about 54% in Wyoming support the President's party more people think that the President has done a bad job.

   8

Part F

1. Reference to aspects of the following will be credited:

   Issue – Poverty in Africa
   - Famine – lack of food supply or ability to afford or grow crops
   - Disease – lack of nutrients, drinking contaminated water (associated illness kills thousands daily)
   - Increased death rates/infant mortality – deaths as a result of malnutrition and associated illnesses
   - Impact on education – poor attendance at school, work instead of learn
   - Impact on economy – less active work force

   Below is a model paragraph answer – 3 marks awarded.

   Poverty in Africa has many consequences for the people of the continent. The poverty experienced by citizens in many African countries is absolute poverty, with many people living below £1 per day, barely having enough to eat or drink in a day. Living in poverty makes people more susceptible to illness and disease.

   6

2. Reference to aspects of the following will be credited:

   Issue – Poverty in Africa
   - A particular case study or example would be useful in this answer, eg Sudan, DR Congo, Somalia, Mali, etc.
   - United Nations – the work of specialised agencies UNICEF, WHO, UNESCO, FAO, WFP. Eg UNICEF: involved in helping meet the specific needs of children. Campaign in southern Africa to prevent AIDS transmission from mothers to children. Campaign to help child soldiers in Sudan
   - Charities and NGO's, eg Oxfam, WaterAid, Christian Aid. Eg Warchild specifically focuses on helping children affected by conflict
   - African Union – increasing co-operation, promoting democracy, human rights and tackling extreme widespread conflict in the continent

   Below is a paragraph model answer – 4 marks awarded.

   International organisations work hard to help those in need in Africa. This help could be in an emergency situation such as during a famine or armed conflict. The United Nations has specialised agencies tasked with helping people in need around the world. UNICEF specifically works to help young people. In Africa

UNICEF works to provide education for those who are not attending school. UNICEF's "Schools for Africa" programme has managed to raise the school enrolment rate in Rwanda to 95% in recent years, up from 74% in 2000.   6

3. You are required to evaluate the sources provided to detect and explain instances of exaggeration and/or selective use of facts, giving developed answers.

   In order to achieve full marks you must include evidence that supports the view and you must include evidence that does not support the view and you must use all three sources.

   An answer which covers only one side of your explanation will be awarded a maximum of 6 marks.

   Below is a model answer – awarded full marks 8/8.

   The first reason Diane Lochrie is selective in her use of facts is when she states "it is obvious that increasing aid reduces poverty in African countries and improves education". Diane is selective as Source 3 shows us that in all of the African countries aid has been increased from 2003 to 2008 but in Source 2 it shows us that poverty has also increased in 4 of the selected countries. Only Ethiopia has seen a slight decrease in poverty levels from 50% to 37%.

   However, Diane was not being selective in stating that aid improves education as Source 2 tells us that literacy rates are increasing in most countries such as in Botswana from 80% to 84% and in Swaziland from 74% to 81%. Only in Zimbabwe has education not improved.

   However, Diane was also being selective in her use of facts when she stated "while those countries with increasing debt are unable to reduce the problem of HIV/AIDS" as Source 3 shows that the debt totals for Botswana, Lesotho, Swaziland and Zimbabwe have increased but Source 1 highlights only Botswana has shown an increase in the percentage of adults living with HIV/AIDS. The other three, have all seen a decrease in the percentage of adults living with HIV/AIDS meaning debt hasn't affected countries' efforts to reduce this problem – for example, 22.1% of adults were living with HIV/Aids in 2003 in Zimbabwe compared to only 15.3% in 2008.   8

NATIONAL 5 MODERN STUDIES MODEL PAPER 3

Section 1

Part A

1. Reference to aspects of the following will be credited:
   - Leader of the Scottish Government
   - Direct policy in the Scottish Government
   - Spokesperson for the Scottish Government
   - Chairs Scottish Cabinet
   - Chooses members of the Scottish Cabinet and other government ministers
   - Leader of the biggest party in the Scottish Parliament
   - Takes part in First Minister's Question Time every week
   - Lead role in discussions with the UK Government
   - Represents Scotland in discussions with other devolved bodies and overseas
   - Focus of media attention

   Below is a model paragraph answer – 3 marks awarded.

   A power of the First Minister is commanding huge media attention. As First Minister you are seen as the figurehead of the Government and you have huge access to the media. An example of the First Minister using this power is when two former SNP MSPs resigned over the party's decision to remain part of NATO should independence happen. Alex Salmond called a press conference and was featured in all major newspapers the next day defending the decision.   6

2. Reference to aspects of the following will be credited:

   Majority government works well
   - Able to put policies into effect
   - Clear, decisive decision making
   - No need to compromise
   - Able to keep election promises

   Majority government does not work well
   - Government may be too powerful and ignore other views
   - Unresponsive to wishes of electorate
   - Unwilling to compromise
   - Able to pursue extreme or unpopular policies

   Below is a model paragraph answer – 4 marks awarded.

   Some people believe majority government works well as the government will be able to carry out their policies. Like the current SNP majority government, long promised policies such as a referendum on independence or a minimum price on alcohol can be put forward by the government. This is good as parties are elected based on the promises in their manifesto so if a government has a majority then they have the right to carry out these policies.   6

3. You are required to evaluate a limited range of sources, detecting and explaining instances of exaggeration and/or selective use of facts, giving developed arguments.

   To achieve full marks you must show evidence that has been selected as it supports the view and show evidence that has not been selected as it does not support the view.

   An answer that deals with only one side of the explanation, or does not use evidence from all sources will only be awarded a maximum of 6 marks.

Below is a model answer – awarded full marks 8/8.

Diana Jones is not being selective when she says "The campaign to end the tolls on the Forth and Tay Bridges had the support of the people of Scotland" as according to Source 1, NAAT lobbied political parties and persuaded the Liberal Democrats to support the scrapping of bridge tolls. This point is backed up by Source 2 as in the Dunfermline and West Fife by-election, the Liberal Democrats won by a massive two thousand majority over Labour.

She is also not being selective as in Source 1 it states that local newspaper the Dundee Courier supported the campaign. This success is further emphasised in Source 3 which states that "tens of thousands" of the public supported the newspaper's campaign by signing petitions, a huge 10,000 people signed online polls and many displayed bumper stickers on their vehicles.

However, Diana Jones is being selective as the campaign did not have the support of the Trade Unions. Source 1 states that the Trade Unions were concerned about the impact on their members. This is backed up by Source 2 which states that the Transport and General Workers Union was concerned over job losses and estimated that 175 of their members faced the sack.   **8**

Part B

1. Reference to aspects of the following will be credited:
   - Leader of the UK Government
   - Direct policy in the UK Government
   - Spokesperson for the UK Government
   - Chairs UK Cabinet
   - Chooses members of the UK Cabinet and other government ministers
   - Leader of the biggest party in the UK Parliament
   - Takes part in Prime Minister's Question Time every week
   - Lead role in discussions with other governments from around the world
   - Focus of media attention

   Below is a model answer – 3 marks awarded.

   A power of the Prime Minister is commanding huge media attention. As Prime Minister you are seen as the figurehead of the Government and you have huge access to the media. An example of the Prime Minister using this power was when there was a terrorist attack in Woolwich. David Cameron called a press conference and was featured in all major newspapers the next day speaking on behalf of the Government condemning the attack.   **6**

2. Reference to aspects of the following will be credited:

   Coalition government works well
   - Parties work together so more cooperation and compromise
   - More voters feel represented in government
   - Unpopular and extreme policies less likely as government needs to maintain support

   Coalition government does not work well
   - Voters dissatisfied as voters generally do not vote for a coalition but for a single party who they wish to see form a government
   - May be unstable as parties find it difficult to work together
   - May be indecisive and unable to take radical but necessary decisions

Below is a model answer – 4 marks awarded.

Some people believe coalition government works well as it means that the government has to work together and cooperate with each other more. As it is important to satisfy more than one political party it means that decisions can't be dominated by one viewpoint. This means that the promises the parties made in their manifestos can be carried out and so more voters are represented in the government. For example, the Liberal Democrats forced a referendum on the voting system and the Conservatives forced a rise in tuition fees.   **6**

3. You are required to evaluate a limited range of sources, detecting and explaining instances of exaggeration and/or selective use of facts, giving developed arguments.

To achieve full marks you must show evidence that has been selected as it supports the view and show evidence that has not been selected as it does not support the view.

An answer that deals with only one side of the explanation, or does not use evidence from all sources will only be awarded a maximum of 6 marks.

Below is a model answer – awarded full marks 8/8.

Chris Knight is not being selective in the use of facts when he says "Compulsory voting would improve democracy and would be popular with voters" as according to Source 1 supporters of compulsory voting say it will increase turnout and allow parties to concentrate on issues leading to more debate. This is backed up by Source 3 in which Brian Davidson MP says it will get more people interested in politics.

However, Chris Knight is being selective in the use of facts as Source 1 claims that some people feel it would be wrong to force people to vote and it would be against British traditions. Indeed according to Source 3 forcing people to vote would lead to more spoilt ballot papers as many people simply do not trust politicians, especially young people who are least likely to vote as only 24% of 18–24 year olds are certain to vote (Source 2).

In addition, he is also being selective as according to Source 1 compulsory voting is not part of UK law and it would be difficult to enforce and a waste of police and court time. Added to the fact that, in Source 3, MP Oliver Heald says there is little support to make it a criminal offence not to vote and he feels the answer is for politicians to excite the electorate.   **8**

Section 2

Part C

1. Reference to aspects of the following will be credited:
   - Lack of success in education
   - Low self-esteem
   - Lack of material goods
   - Overcrowded/low standard of housing
   - Poor diet
   - Ill health
   - Breakdown of family

   Below is a model paragraph answer – 3 marks awarded.

   If a child is living in poverty they may suffer poorer health than other children who don't live in poverty. This can be to do with the fact that a child living in poverty may have a poor diet of cheap foods such as tinned or ready meals. With fruit and vegetables being expensive, parents can't afford to buy and feed their children healthier foods every day.   **4**

2. Reference to aspects of the following will be credited:

Government policies
- Increase access to health care by increased spending
- Free prescriptions
- Health promotion and prevention campaigns
- Legal measures, eg smoking ban/minimum alcohol pricing
- Measures restricting drink promotions

Individual actions
- Better/more healthy diet, eg more fruit and vegetables
- More exercise, eg regular walking, join a gym
- Smoking – reduce or stop entirely
- Alcohol – moderate consumption
- Drugs – give up use of drugs

Below is a model paragraph answer – 4 marks awarded.

> The Government tries to improve the health of the general population in various ways. Firstly, the Government can introduce new laws that it believes will make people healthier. For example, in 2006 the Government introduced the smoking ban. This prevented people from smoking in public places such as in bars and restaurants. This has led to many people stopping smoking and fewer suffering illness through passive smoking. Due to the smoking ban, rates of cancer have fallen and the health of the population has improved. **6**

3. You must use a limited range of sources by selecting evidence from them in order to make and justify a decision/recommendation.

You will be awarded up to three marks for a justification depending on relevance and development of the evidence.

You will be highly credited if you make justifications which show interaction between the sources.

For full marks, you must justify your decision/recommendation and explain why you have rejected the other option. Answers, which deal with only one decision, will be awarded a maximum of eight marks.

Across the whole answer you must use all 3 sources to achieve full marks.

Below is a model answer – awarded full marks 10/10.

> In my role as Scottish Government advisor I have decided to recommend Option 2, to scrap the scheme which pays smokers to stop smoking.
>
> My first reason for this is highlighted in Source 1 where is states that "many NHS staff think that other methods such as nicotine gum are more effective in helping smokers to give up cigarettes." This links in with Source 3 where Maria Logan states "alternatives such as nicotine gum and patches have proved to work in the long run."
>
> Another reason to choose Option 2 is shown in Source 2 where the percentage success rate of counselling tell us that people who have been given 91–300 minutes of counselling have a 27% success rate of stopping smoking. This links with Source 2 which states "long-term counselling has proven to be a very effective method." Source 1 also tells us that "payments will be made for a maximum of 12 weeks" with Maria Logan highlighting in Source 3 that "it is unrealistic to expect people to give up for good after only 12 weeks." This, therefore, renders the scheme pointless.

> A final reason to choose Option 2 is from Source 1 which states that "some local people say it is unfair that smokers are getting extra money while others living in poverty get nothing." Maria Logan backs this up in Source 3 when she states "Many non-smoking families are living in poverty, but they are not being paid £12.50 extra a week to help with their shopping."
>
> I did not choose Option 1, to extend the scheme which pays smokers to stop smoking across the whole of Scotland, as although Source 1 states "it is hoped 1800 smokers will sign up for the project" Source 1 also highlights that in fact "after 3 months only 360 people had signed up to the project in Dundee." The scheme, therefore, isn't popular and should be scrapped. **10**

Part D

1. Reference to aspects of the following will be credited:
- Maintain law and order, eg police on the beat
- Detect crimes, eg carry out investigations, interview witnesses, process evidence
- Crime prevention, eg visiting schools, Neighbourhood Watch
- Protection of the public, eg security at football matches
- Initiatives, eg knife amnesties
- Involvement in Court System

Below is a model paragraph answer – 3 marks awarded.

> The main role of the police is to maintain law and order in society. They do this in a variety of different ways. Firstly, the police will work on crime prevention. In doing this they will observe the public and patrol on the beat. The police will also visit schools and give presentations on issues such as drug and knife crime. Through crime prevention the rate of criminal activity is greatly reduced. **4**

2. Reference to aspects of the following will be credited:
- Prison is not effective especially for short sentences
- High level of recidivism leading to many questioning effectiveness of prison
- Relatively few opportunities for rehabilitation
- Prisons are expensive and overcrowded
- Success of drug courts in rehabilitating offenders
- Electronic tags less expensive than prison
- Success of restorative justice especially for young offenders

Below is a model paragraph answer – 4 marks awarded.

> Scottish courts often decide to use alternative punishments to prison. The first reason for this is that Scotland's prisons are already overcrowded. Instead of putting a criminal in jail for a short sentence, a community service punishment or a fine may be more appropriate and it solves the issue of overcrowding the prison system which in turn leads to a poor standard of living for prisoners, stress on prison staff and unwanted negative media attention on the prison service. **6**

3. You must use a limited range of sources by selecting evidence from them in order to make and justify a decision/recommendation.

You will be awarded up to three marks for a justification depending on relevance and development of the evidence.

You will be highly credited if you make justifications which show interaction between the sources.

For full marks, you must justify your decision/recommendation and explain why you have rejected the other option. Answers, which deal with only one decision, will be awarded a maximum of eight marks.

Across the whole answer you must use all 3 sources to achieve full marks.

Below is a model answer – awarded full marks 10/10.

> In my role as government advisor I have decided to recommend Option 2 that the government should not install more CCTV cameras.
>
> My first reason for recommending Option 2 is found in Source 1 which states "some research indicates where cameras are installed crime increases in nearby areas without CCTV cameras." This is backed up by Source 3 where Pauline Clark states "at best, CCTV only makes offenders move away from areas with cameras to commit crimes where there are none." Installing more cameras will only continue this trend.
>
> Another reason to choose Option 2 is found in Source 3 where Pauline Clark states that "installing CCTV does not reduce crime rates." Source 1 backs this up stating "a case study in the Greater Glasgow area could find no link between the installation of CCTV cameras and a reduction in crime." Figures from source 2 proves this showing that after CCTV was installed in an inner city estate crimes actually increased by 14%. This means installing more CCTV would be pointless.
>
> A final reason to back up my recommendation is found in Source 1 where it states that "many members of the public are concerned that more CCTV cameras means a loss of civil liberties and an invasion of privacy." This is backed up by source 2 where it shows 36% of people believed CCTV was an invasion of privacy. Pauline Clark also states in Source 3 "CCTV is an invasion of privacy as most ordinary citizens do not commit crimes but still have their movements followed and recorded up to 300 times per day." The last thing we need is more CCTV cameras following innocent people.
>
> The reason I didn't choose Option 1 is although John Morton states "CCTV can save tax payers money by speeding up court cases" Source 1 states "Scotland's cities already have too many cameras in operation compared to other countries, costing huge amounts of money."   **10**

Section 3

Part E

1. Reference to aspects of the following will be credited:
   - The right to vote in local and national elections
   - The right to freedom of speech in public and online
   - The right to protest
   - The responsibility to turn out and use the vote
   - The responsibility to use speech sensibly with specific reference to a G20 country's control
   - The responsibility to ensure that protests are government approved

Below is a model paragraph answer – awarded 3 marks.

> The country I have studied is China. One right people have in China is the right to use the Internet to find out information or communicate with other. However, a responsibility is to avoid websites that are banned by the Government and to avoid discussing politics in a negative way. An example of a website which is banned in China is Facebook.   **6**

2. Reference to aspects of the following will be credited:
   - Educational issues in your selected country
   - Any issues relating to health care and inequalities within your selected country
   - Issues relating to law and order within your selected country
   - Differences in housing between different groups in your selected country

Below is a model paragraph answer – 4 marks awarded.

> The country I have studied is China. In China there are inequalities between the poor rural communities and the rich urban areas. In the rural areas people have less access to well paid jobs as the work is mainly local and agricultural. Whereas in urban areas workers have access to large Chinese and multinational businesses where the wages are usually much higher. Especially in Special Economic Zones such as Hong Kong. For example, Foxconn, the company who assembles Apple products pays their workers almost double the average wage within China.   **6**

3. You are required to use the sources provided to draw valid conclusions, with supporting evidence.

You should draw conclusions using the headings/bullet points in the question.

An answer which merely repeats the source material without making judgements or conclusions will be awarded zero marks.

For full marks three developed conclusions must be given.

You should link information within and between sources in support of your conclusions.

The conclusion can be placed either at the beginning or at the end after the evidence.

Below is a model answer – awarded full marks 8/8.

> ### HIV/AIDS in mothers and children
>
> The conclusion is there has been good progress in the treatment of mothers and children with HIV/AIDS.
>
> According to Source 1 the number of pregnant women on antiretroviral treatment (ART) which prevents mother to child transmission of HIV, almost doubled between 2007 and 2008. ART is now available to over 50% of those in need. In addition, the percentage of pregnant women who are HIV positive receiving ART has steadily increased since 2004 according to Source 3.
>
> ### Provincial Differences
>
> The Conclusion is that provincial differences remain in those who are dying from HIV/AIDS.
>
> In Source 2 it shows that the number of people who die due to AIDS is much higher in some regions such as KwaZulu, whereas in other regions such as the Western Cape the number is much lower. This corresponds to the information in Source 1 which shows that as some areas have a greater number of those with HIV/AIDS, this has reduced the life expectancy in some Provinces.
>
> ### How effective the Government is in dealing with HIV/AIDS
>
> The conclusion is that the Government is taking the problem more seriously and is increasing spending to try to tackle the problem.
>
> Source 1 states the UN report found that the South African Government's plan to tackle HIV/AIDS was one of the largest treatment programmes in the world. This

corresponds with Source 3 in which the percentage of women of are HIV receiving ART has increased year on year and has risen from 15% in 2004 to 73% in 2008. **8**

Part F

1. Reference to aspects of the following will be credited:

   Issue – War
   - Child soldiers
   - Orphans
   - Refugees
   - Breakdown of society
   - Lack of education
   - Political unrest

   Below is a model paragraph answer – 3 marks awarded.

   > The consequences of war on the population of a country can be devastating. Children can be recruited to fight in wars as child soldiers which can lead to children being killed or killing other people. Child soldiers are treated terribly by their captors and can often be physically and mentally abused. This has happened in many African countries such as Sudan and Mali. **4**

2. Reference to aspects of the following will be credited:

   Issue: Poverty in Africa
   - Political corruption or instability
   - Debt
   - Lack of infrastructure
   - Armed conflict
   - Trade issues
   - Natural disasters – famine, floods, etc.

   Below is a model paragraph answer – 4 marks awarded.

   > It can be very difficult tackling poverty in Africa due to corruption in politics. Developed nations and charities may donate aid to a country in the hope that it will help the poor and suffering in that country, however, it has been the case in the past in Africa that government officials have stolen aid money or misspent it meaning the aid does not filter through to the needy. The current leader of Sudan, Omar al-Bashir, has been accused of siphoning aid money and has expelled aid agencies from the country over the years. **6**

3. You are required to use the sources provided to draw valid conclusions, with supporting evidence.

   You should draw conclusions using the headings/bullet points in the question.

   An answer which merely repeats the source material without making judgements or conclusions will be awarded zero marks.

   For full marks three developed conclusions must be given.

   You should link information within and between sources in support of your conclusions.

   The conclusion can be placed either at the beginning or at the end after the evidence.

   Below is a model answer – awarded full marks 8/8.

   Changes in the level of terrorist incidents worldwide

   > My first conclusion is that the number of terrorist related incidents has declined in recent years. Source 1 states "the number of terrorist related incidents worldwide dropping from a high in 2008 to a low in 2012." This links with Source 2 which shows that in 2008 there were 13,435 incidents and in 2012 there was only 10,138 highlighting a significant decline.

   Motives behind terrorist incidents in selected countries

   > The conclusion is that religion is the most common cause of terrorist incidents. This is supported by evidence from Source 3 which shows political reasons are the main cause of terrorism in the USA but religion is the main cause in Afghanistan, Pakistan and Somalia with hundreds of incidents in these countries. This links in with Source 1 which states "In Afghanistan, Pakistan and Somalia the most common motive for terror was religious reasons."

   The levels of terrorist incidents in selected countries

   > My conclusion is that the level of terrorist incidents is decreasing in some countries but increasing in others. This is supported by evidence firstly from Source 1 which states "The amount of incidents in individual countries has also come down with the amount in Afghanistan decreasing. However, the number of terrorist incidents in Somalia and Spain has increased which is a worrying trend." This links with Source 2 which shows in 2010 Afghanistan suffered 956 terrorist incidents then in 2012 suffered fewer with 912. Source 2 also shows the increase in Spain and Somalia – Spain increasing by 2 and Somalia by 49. **8**

NATIONAL 5 MODERN STUDIES 2014

Section 1

Part A : Democracy in Scotland

1. *Candidates can be credited in a number of ways **up to a maximum of 6 marks**.*

Possible approaches to answering the question:

The Scottish Parliament has control over devolved powers in Scotland like health, education and housing.
[2 marks for a list answer which lacks any detail]

The Scottish Parliament has a range of devolved powers. One of the main ones is education. Scottish pupils sit Nationals and Highers whereas English students sit GCSEs.
[2 marks single point with an example]

Holyrood has control over many devolved areas such as health care. The Scottish government has been able to create different laws in Scotland eg the Smoking Ban in 2006 and the plan to have a minimum price for alcohol.
[3 marks developed point with exemplification]

Reference to aspects of the following will be credited:
• The power to make law
• Agriculture, forestry and fishing
• Education & training
• Health & social services
• Housing
• Law & order

2. *Candidates can be credited in a number of ways **up to a maximum of 6 marks**.*

Possible approaches to answering the question:

People may feel it is their right to vote and that they should therefore use it.
[1 mark for a limited answer which lacks any detail.]

Many people are members of political parties such as the Scottish National Party and so vote for their candidate.
[2 marks for a single point with an example]

Many people in Scotland feel that it is not only a right but also a responsibility that they should vote to uphold democracy. If many thousands of Scots decide not to vote then the result of an election may not be representative. In 2011 almost 40% didn't vote, if they had, the SNP may not have won.
[3 marks for a developed point with exemplification]

Reference to aspects of the following will be credited:
• Basic right in a democracy
• Right denied to citizens elsewhere in the world
• Desire to see own party succeed
• Wish to ensure another party is not elected.
• Right denied to women until early last century
• Feel electoral system reflects their views

3. *Candidates can be credited in a number of ways **up to a maximum of 8 marks**.*

Possible approaches to answering the question:

The importance of Trade Union donations to party election campaigns.

Conclusion – Trade Union contributions were not very important to political parties during the election in 2011. [1 mark for valid conclusion]

Evidence – Trade Unions contributed 29% of the overall donations to political parties in 2011 compared to 41% from individuals [Source 3]
The SNP and Conservatives rely more on wealthy business people and as such unions are not important to them [Source 1]

Conclusion – They are much more important to Labour than the other parties [1 mark for valid conclusion]

Evidence – 29% is almost a third of all party donations – Labour however is more reliant as over a third of their funding is from trade unions (36%). [Sources 1 and 3]

The link between a party's election spending and election success.

Conclusion – The party which spends the most wins the election. [1 mark for a valid conclusion]

Evidence – In 2007, SNP spent the most at c£3.5 million compared to Labour at £1.6 million [Source 2] and they won the election by 1 seat [Source 3]
In 2011, SNP spent the most at c£2.6 million compared to Labour's £1.1 million [Source 2] and the SNP won 69 seats compared to 37 for Labour [Source 3].

The link between election spending and voter awareness of election campaign methods.

Conclusion – There is a direct link between election spending and voter awareness of campaign methods. [1 mark for valid conclusion]

Evidence – Spending on leaflets increased from £1.2 million to £1.4 million between 2007 and 2011 and awareness of leaflets increased from 89% to 93% of voters. [Source 1]

Conclusion – Money spent on campaign methods means people are more aware of it. [1 mark for valid conclusion]

Evidence – In 2011, the smallest sum (only £47,000) was spent on rallies and public meetings and only 2% of people attended these (this is the smallest number). [Source 1]

Part B : Democracy in the United Kingdom

1. *Candidates can be credited in a number of ways **up to a maximum of 6 marks**.*

Possible approaches to answering the question:

The UK Parliament has reserved powers in Scotland like defence and immigration.
[1 mark for a list answer which lacks any detail]

One of the main reserved powers is the benefit system eg child benefit is the same in Edinburgh and London.
[2 marks for a single point with an example]

The UK Parliament has a range of reserved powers which affect Scotland. One of these is defence. The UK government has power over the size and location of Scottish forces eg in 2013 Leuchars air base was reduced in size and changed to an army base.
[3 marks for a developed point with exemplification]

Reference to aspects of the following will be credited:
• The power to make law
• Immigration
• Benefits & social security
• Defence
• Foreign policy
• Nuclear power

2. *Candidates can be credited in a number of ways **up to a maximum of 6 marks**.*

Possible approaches to answering the question:

People may feel it is their right to vote and that they should therefore use it.
          [1 mark for a limited answer which lacks any detail.]

Many people are members of political parties such as the Labour Party and so vote for their candidate.
          [2 marks for a single point with an example]

Many people in the UK feel that it is not only a right but also a responsibility that they should vote to uphold democracy. If many thousands of Scots decide not to vote then the result of an election may not be representative. Eg In 2010 approx one third of people didn't vote in the general election. If they had, the coalition may not have been necessary.
          [3 marks for a developed point with exemplification]

Reference to aspects of the following will be credited:
• Basic right in a democracy
• People likely to participate in a General Election
• Right denied to citizens elsewhere in the world
• Desire to see own party succeed
• Wish to ensure another party is not elected
• Right denied to women until early last century

3. *Candidates can be credited in a number of ways **up to a maximum of 8 marks**.*

Possible approaches to answering the question:

The importance of trade union donations to party election campaigns.

Conclusion – trade union contributions were not very important to political parties during the election in 2010.
          [1 mark for valid conclusion]

Evidence –
Trade unions contributed 16% of the overall donations to political parties in 2010 compared to 47% from individuals [Source 3]
The Labour Party received 36% of their funding from Unions but this is less than half so not that important [Source 1]
The Conservatives rely on wealthy business people so Unions are not important to them [Source 1]

Conclusion – trade unions are more important to Labour than the other parties. [1 mark valid conclusion]

Evidence –
16% of all party donations [Source 3]
Labour however is more reliant as over a third of their funding is from trade unions (36%) [Source 1]

The link between a party's election spending and election success.

Conclusion – The party which spends the most wins the election. [1 mark valid conclusion]

Evidence –
In 2005 Labour spent the most at c£18 million compared to Conservatives at £17 million [Source 2] and they won the election by 158 seats [Source 3]
In 2010 Conservatives spent the most at c£16 million compared to Labour's £8 million [Source 2] and the Conservatives won 307 seats compared to 258 for Labour [Source 3].

The link between election spending and voter awareness of election campaign methods.

Conclusion – As election spending on campaign methods decreases so does voter awareness of these methods [1 mark valid conclusion]

Evidence – In 2005, £15 million was spent on billboard advertising and this fell to £9 million in 2010 [Source 1] Awareness of billboard advertising fell from 62% in 2005 to 48% in 2010. [Source 1]

Conclusion – More money spent on a campaign method means people are more aware of it, eg leaflets [1 mark valid conclusion]

Evidence – In 2010, most money (£12.3 million) was spent on leaflets and 93% of people had received leaflets. [Source 1]
Only 1.7 million was spent on public meetings and only 2% of people attended one in 2010 [Source 1]

Section 2

Part C : Social Inequality

1. *Candidates can be credited in a number of ways **up to a maximum of 4 marks**.*

Possible approaches to answering the question:

The Government has tried to tackle inequality by providing benefits.
          [1 mark – accurate but undeveloped point]

The Government has tried to tackle inequality by providing more apprenticeships.
          [1 mark – accurate but undeveloped point]

The Voluntary sector has tried to tackle inequality by providing financial support to vulnerable groups such as children. Cash for Kids is a children's charity that raises money for disadvantaged children.
          [2 marks – accurate with development]

The Government has introduced the Universal Credit to tackle inequality. This benefit was introduced in October 2013. Universal Credit is a single payment that merges a number of benefits together to make them easier to claim. For example, Universal Credit helps to pay childcare costs and allow parents to work.
          [3 marks – accurate point with development and exemplification]

GOVERNMENT
• **All major benefits provided by Central Government including:** Universal Credit; Attendance Allowance; Disability Living Allowance, Carers Allowance etc
• **Elderly Benefits:** Pension Credits; Winter Fuel payment; Cold Weather Payments and free TV Licence for over 75yrs
• **Council Tax Benefit:** Helps to meet the financial needs of low income groups by providing a reduction in their Council Tax bill
• **Families:** Free School Meals; School Clothing vouchers, Maternity Allowance and Educational Maintenance Allowance (EMA)
• **Disability Living Allowance** (Known from April 2013 as Person Independence Payments): Paid to those under 65 who have extra costs created by a disability
• **Recent legislation** e.g. Childcare Act [2006], Equality Act [2010]

INDIVIDUALS
- Taking individual responsibility for circumstances
- Working hard at school, college & university
- Undertaking voluntary work to gain skills/experience
- Contributing to charity – altruistic actions
- Setting a good example for peers/friends/family
- Making full use of government help eg training schemes or Job Centre Plus

VOLUNTARY SECTOR
- **Charities:** groups such as Barnardo's, Enable Scotland, Glasgow's Children's Holiday Scheme or Glasgow the Caring City who help the most vulnerable in society
- **Housing Associations:** Non-profit making organisations that provide low cost social housing
- **Credit Unions:** Providing low cost loans and mortgages to its members

PRIVATE SECTOR
- **Retail/Shops:** Providing special discount days for vulnerable groups eg B&Q Pensioners discount
- **Leisure Facilities:** Concession and reduced gym membership rates for students, pensioners and families. Special family meals deal in restaurants
- **Private Schools/Nurseries:** Reduced fees for more than one child
- **Supermarkets:** Introduction of low cost/value brand fruit and vegetables

2. *Candidates can be credited in a number of ways **up to a maximum of 8 marks.***

Possible approaches to answering the question:

Some people live in poverty because they don't have a job.

[1 mark – accurate but undeveloped point]

Some people live in poverty because they have lost their job because of a recession.

[2 marks – accurate point with development]

Some people live in poverty because they lack qualifications. This might be because they did not try hard at school and did not pass any exams. This makes it harder for them to find a job that is well paid, so might only be able to get work in lower paid jobs such as working in a shop.

[3 marks – accurate point with development and exemplification]

Some people live in poverty because of their family type. For example, a lone parent family may be more at risk from poverty than a family that has two working parents. Also many lone parent families are headed by women who tend to get paid less than men. Lone parents might live in poverty because they are dependent on benefits as it might be difficult for them to find work with hours suitable or pay for childcare when working.

[4 marks – relevant, accurate point with development, analysis and exemplification]

Reference to aspects of the following will be credited:
- **Occupations:** Some people have well-paid jobs such as professionals, while others may work in lower paid occupations
- **Recession:** Some people might lose their jobs during a recession. The jobs that are normally affected first are lower paid service sector jobs
- **Long term unemployment:** Some groups such as NEETs may never have had a job, and subsequently find it difficult to get a job without experience so remain on benefits and unemployed

- **Educational attainment:** Some people leave school with no or few qualifications, which means they cannot enter further or higher education. This means that they don't have the same earning potential as someone who has gone to college or university so will generally be paid less
- **Household Structure:** A household with one adult is more likely to live in poverty than a household with two adults
- **Lack of skills:** Some people, for example the elderly, may not have skills appropriate to the job market, eg IT skills, so find it difficult to find employment
- **Ill health:** Some people may have long term health problems that mean they cannot work or have to give up work because of poor health, eg cancer sufferers
- **Social problems:** Some people experience social problems such as addictions to drugs and alcohol that may affect their ability to find or hold down a stable job. Other social problems such as involvement in crime may push a person into poverty if they have a criminal record they might find it harder to get a job
- **Race:** Ethnic minorities still experience prejudice and discrimination. Those with language difficulties might find it difficult to get a job, and therefore have difficulty accessing a decent level of income. Poverty rates amongst ethnic minorities are higher than whites
- **Gender:** More women work part-time or in lower paid jobs. Also wage inequality means women are paid on average 15% less than men, so lowering their earning potential
- **Age and disability:** The elderly have higher poverty rates as many rely solely on the state retirement pension. Disability poverty levels are also higher than average poverty rates as 30% of disabled adults live in poverty compared to 20% of the overall adult population

3. *Candidates can be credited in a number of ways **up to a maximum of 8 marks.***

Possible approaches to answering the question:

Sophie Wilson is supported (not selective) in her view **"There have been great improvements in the UK's health in the last 10 years."**

Candidates should give evidence from the Sources that supports Sophie Wilson's view.

Sophie's view is supported (not selective) by Source 1 which shows that life expectancy has increased.

[1 mark – accurate use of Source 1 but minimal development]

Sophie's view is supported (not selective) by Source 1 which shows that life expectancy has increased in the last 10 years from 77 years to 80 years because we are making better lifestyle choices.

[2 marks – accurate use of Source 1 and detailed use of statistics]

Sophie's view is supported (not selective) by Source 1 which shows people are making better lifestyles choices. This is supported by Source 2 that shows the number of people smoking has decreased by 5% for both men and women in the last 10 years. This has also led to a decrease in the number of heart attacks associated with smoking. This shows that the UK's health has improved.

[3 marks – accurate information from two Sources with some evaluation of the statistics, ie '..this shows the UK's health has improved.']

Reference to aspects of the following will be credited:
- People are eating healthier and exercising more (Source 1)
- Big decrease in death rates compared to other countries (Source 1)
- Smoking rates for men and women have fallen (Source 2) because Government outlawed smoking in public places (Source 3)
- The number of admissions to hospitals has decreased, these include children's asthmas admissions from 26,969 cases in 2006 to 20,167 cases in 2013 (Source 3)
- The Government has worked hard to improve the health of the nation (Source 1) by passing laws banning smoking in public places (Source 3)

Sophie Wilson is opposed (selective) in her view **"There have been great improvements in the UK's health in the last 10 years."**

Candidates should give evidence from the Sources that oppose Sophie Wilson's view.

Sophie's view is opposed (selective) as Source 1 shows many doctors warn that more has to be done to tackle the growing problem of childhood obesity and the health problems it causes. This is supported by Source 2 that shows the number of adults who are classed as obese has also risen over the last 10 years, with a 5% increase in Scotland and a 4% increase in England. This shows that health relating to obesity has not improved over the last 10 years.

[3 marks – accurate information from two Sources with some evaluation of the statistics, ie '..this shows Britain's health has not improved..']

Reference to aspects of the following will be credited:
- Source 1 shows that obesity is a big problem in the UK
- Britain's health still poor compared with other Western European Countries (Source 1)
- Since 2004, the number of obese children suffering from diabetes has doubled (Source 1)
- Obesity rates in Scotland and in England are increasing (Source 2)
- Approximately one in five adults continue to smoke in the UK (Source 3), with male smoking rates constantly higher than female rates (Source 2)
- Source 3 shows that people are still making bad health choices, especially in Scotland with 27% of adults smoking and up to 40% in deprived inner city areas. (Source 3)

Part D : Crime and the Law

1. *Candidates can be credited in a number of ways **up to a maximum of 4 marks**.*

Possible approaches to answering the question:

The Children's Hearing System can help young people by taking them away from their home. (1 mark)

The Children's Hearing System tries to deal with the reasons why young people commit crime and offers support for them to stop offending. (2 marks)

The Children's Hearing System helps young people by providing a relaxed atmosphere where young people can discuss their offending behaviour. It is less intimidating than going to an adult court and they will get help and support from school, social workers and the police to change their behaviour. (3 marks)

Reference to aspects of the following will be credited:
- Targets both offending behaviour and welfare concerns
- Impartial, voluntary panel makes decisions
- Safe environment to discuss issues and problems
- Tries to deal with root cause of problems
- Input from various agencies eg police, social work, schools
- Power to remove "at risk" children from their homes
- Can refer to secure accommodation or court if necessary

2. *Candidates can be credited in a number of ways **up to a maximum of 8 marks**.*

Possible approaches to answering the question:

Prisons don't reduce reoffending because you learn how to commit more crimes when you are inside. (1 mark)

Electronic tags are a good way of reducing reoffending as if you have a job you can still go but are punished with a curfew at night (2 marks)

Many prisons don't have enough staff or money to run effective rehabilitation programmes which means that some offenders are released with the same addictions they had when they went in to prison. (3 marks)

Community Service Orders have been very successful in reducing reoffending as they make the offender pay something back to the community. This could involve painting a children's playground which makes the offender feel they have done something good that others will benefit from. This can change the negative feelings many offenders have and give them back some pride and self-esteem which will make them less likely to commit another crime. (4 marks)

Reference to aspects of the following will be credited:
- High levels of re-offending lead to belief that prison doesn't work
- Prisons are expensive and overcrowded
- Few opportunities for rehabilitation in prisons
- Success of Drug Courts and Drug Treatment and Testing Orders (DTTOs)
- Electronic tagging allows offenders to stay at home, continue working and maintain family relationships
- Success of Community Service Orders (CSOs)
- High levels of success for Restorative Justice especially among young people and first-time offenders
- Too many short sentences which fail to rehabilitate as well as a community sentence would

3. *Candidates can be credited in a number of ways **up to a maximum of 8 marks**.*

Possible approaches to answering the question:

Oliver Thomson is supported (not selective) in his view, "Victims of crime in Scotland receive satisfactory support."

Candidates should give evidence from the Sources that support Oliver Thomson's view.

Oliver Thomson's view is supported (not selective) because it says Surveys show that victims are satisfied with the help and support given to them as victims of crime. This is supported by Source two which says that 69% of victims are happy with police support and further that 74% were happy with Victim Support Scotland. Both of these figures show a significant majority of victims who are satisfied. (3 marks—accurate information from two parts of Source 2 with some evaluative terminology used regarding the statistic included, ie "significant majority")

Reference to aspects of the following will be credited:
- Victim Support Scotland (VSS) is a voluntary group which provides a listening service for victims. Their volunteers can be easily contacted by phone, email or face to face (Source 1)
- The Victims and Witnesses Bill, proposes a "victim surcharge", meaning that those who commit crimes will contribute to the cost of providing support to victims eg house alarm systems and travel costs to hospital (Source 1 and 3)
- Over £5 million per year is provided by the Scottish Government to support Victim Support Scotland and they have committed to maintaining that level of funding (Source 1)
- The Scottish Government has made a very positive attempt to support victims of crime in introducing the Victim and Witness Bill (Source 3)
- Victims on the whole are happy with the support they get from voluntary groups and the police (Source 3)

Oliver Thomson is opposed (selective) in his view, "Victims of crime in Scotland receive satisfactory support."

Candidates should give evidence from the Sources that oppose Oliver Thomson's view.

Oliver's view is opposed (selective) as the Scottish Victim Crisis Centre is a voluntary group which has a 9 month waiting list for victims who wish to talk about their experiences of crime (1 mark – accurate use of Source 1 but no development).

Oliver's view is opposed (selective) as the Scottish Victim Crisis Centre is a voluntary group which has a 9 month waiting list for victims who wish to talk about their experiences of crime. This is supported by Source 3 which says the funding given to some voluntary groups is simply not enough to support the level of demand for services such as counselling and advice. (2 marks – evidence linked from Sources 1 and 3).

Reference to aspects of the following will be credited:
- Victim Support volunteers are not trained counsellors and can only give practical information (Source 1)
- Funding is so low in the Scottish Victim Crisis Centre that victims often get an engaged tone or an answering machine (Source 1)
- The Scottish Government give the Scottish Victim Crisis Centre £50,000 a year but staff say this is nowhere near enough to meet the demand for their services (Source 1)
- The funding given to some voluntary groups is simply not enough to support the level of demand for services such as counselling and advice (Source 3)
- Some voluntary groups are not able to give full training to their staff as they can't afford it (Source 3)

Section 3

Part E : World Powers

1. *Candidates can be credited in a number of ways **up to a maximum of 4 marks**.*

Possible approaches to answering the question:

USA
- In America, Barack Obama introduced a new health-care law
                              [1 mark – accurate point]
- In America, Barack Obama introduced a new health-care law to try and help poor people get health care
                              [2 marks – developed point]

- In America, Barack Obama introduced a new health-care law called the Affordable Care Act. Lots of Americans cannot afford private health care, especially people on low incomes who tend to be ethnic minorities. The act forces people to get health care or they will be fined
              [3 marks – accurate point with development and exemplification]

Reference to aspects of the following will be credited:
- Medicare, Medicaid and State Children's Health Insurance Program (covers children who do not qualify for Medicaid)
- Temporary Assistance for Needy Families (TANF)
- Affirmative Action programmes as they apply today eg the Supreme Court has basically ruled that consideration of an applicant's race/ethnicity is legal
- American Recovery and Reinvestment Act 2009 – provides expansion of unemployment benefits, social welfare provision, education and health care
- No Child Left Behind (NCLB) 2001 – aimed to improve performance in public schools to improve qualifications/employability of all children. Backed with big increases in federal funding but on-going debate as to success
- Race to the Top is a $4.35 billion United States Department of Education contest created to spur innovation and reforms in state and local district education. It is funded as part of the American Recovery and Reinvestment Act of 2009
- Food stamps now known as Supplemental Nutrition Assistance Programme (SNAP) to provide healthy food for poor families
- Federal minimum wage

CHINA
- Today most farms operate as private businesses and decisions about what to produce and how to produce are made by farmers. The government created the Household Responsibility System. Farmers have to give a certain amount to the government, but any surplus is kept by the farmer. This means that poor farmers are allowed to sell their goods for a profit thus reducing inequality
              [3 marks – accurate point with development and exemplification]

Reference to aspects of the following will be credited:
- Dismantling of work permit system (hukou)
- Foreign investment, encouragement of private business (Open Door Policy and Special Economic Zones)
- Encouraging rural areas and small towns to develop entrepreneurs and industrial growth (Township and Village Enterprises)
- Development of social security system
- Better rights for women
- Improving health services, housing and reducing crime

SOUTH AFRICA
Reference to aspects of the following will be credited:
- Affirmative Action
- Black Economic Empowerment (BEE)
- Programmes to ensure everyone has access to drinkable water, sanitation and electricity
- Land redistribution policy

2. *Candidates can be credited in a number of ways **up to a maximum of 6 marks**.*

Possible approaches to answering the question:

USA
Participation of Hispanics is unequal due to language barriers.

[1 mark – accurate point]

Participation of African Americans/Hispanics is unequal because levels of representation are poor especially at Federal Government level. This leads to a lack of positive ethnic minority role models. Some limited progress has been made, eg election of Barack Obama but there have been 43 white Presidents and only 1 black president. Many African/Hispanic Americans simply view politics as a "a white man's game".

[4 marks – relevant, accurate point with development, analysis and exemplification]

- Many ethnic minorities feel their vote doesn't matter as they have not seen much improvement in their living conditions/economic position
- Relationship between participation and poorer levels of education
- Growing up in poor conditions, leads to lower levels of engagement with politics so they are less likely to vote, stand as candidates, join political parties
- Hispanics: English might not be their main language but the language of politics is English. Cannot access political debate, campaigns, etc
- The process of registering to vote can be time-consuming, and varies from state to state. It is easy to be confused or put off by the registration forms

Participation of women:
- Traditional view of women as mother, home maker means women don't see politics as a career. Do not have the same level of political ambition/ feel they have to choose one or the other. These views are prevalent amongst religious groups.
- More likely to be lone parents so have other issues to concern them.
- Lack of positive role models.
- Media coverage of female politicians puts some women off, eg Sarah Palin's and Hilary Clinton's treatment by the press was viewed as sexist with too much focus on appearance.

CHINA
- Membership of the Communist Party is strictly controlled and is not an option for many groups (One – Party system)
- Citizens can only vote at local level. Only candidates and parties sanctioned by the Communist Party are allowed to seek election. Eight other parties are legal but do not act as "opposition" eg China Democratic League, Chinese Peasants' and Workers' Democratic Party
- Organisations that have opposed the Communist Party have been banned as dangerous and subversive, eg China Democracy Party, National Democratic Party of Tibet
- Organisations like the Falun Gong and the independence movements for Taiwan and Tibet have also been banned and their members persecuted
- Some pressure group activity is allowed but it cannot question the authority or legitimacy of the Communist Party. Many dissidents have been in prison since Tiananmen Square and others have been exiled eg Wei Jingshen

- Independent trade unions are not permitted. The Federation of Trade Unions is linked to the Communist Party. There has been some limited progress eg improved pay and conditions for Apple workers
- Environmental groups have grown in number eg many campaigned against the building of the Three Gorges Dam. These groups have experienced limited success and have become popular
- Discrimination stops many women taking part in politics. Attitudes have been slow to change and few women stand as candidates. The All-China Women's Federation (linked to Communist Party) campaigns to promote equality

3. *Candidates can be credited in a number of ways **up to a maximum of 10 marks**.*

Possible approaches to answering the question:

OPTION 1
Australia should keep compulsory voting as more people vote.

[1 mark – evidence from Source 1]

Source 1 points out that compulsory voting is widely supported among Australian people and the pie chart shows 65% do not want to get rid of it.

[2 marks – evidence linked from Source 1 and Source 3]

Turnout is higher in Australia with compulsory voting- it was only 47% before it was introduced and now it is around 95% – supported by evidence in Source 2 where turnout at the most recent parliamentary election was 93.22%. Turnout has doubled since it was introduced.

[3 marks – evaluative terminology, evidence linked from Source 1 and 2]

Reference to aspects of the following will be credited:
- The Australian Prime Minister wants to keep compulsory voting (Source 3).
- Result is more accurate when everyone has participated (Source 3).

Reasons for rejecting the other option:

In all countries where there is compulsory voting, turnout is much higher compared to all countries where there isn't eg Brazil and Argentina have turnout rates near 80% while Canada and Russia have only 60%.

[3 marks – detailed evidence with evaluative comments from Source 2]

OPTION 2
Australia should get rid of compulsory voting as it is undemocratic to force people to vote.

[1 mark – evidence from Source 1]

People with little interest in politics are forced to the polls (Source 1) and (Source 3). "People who aren't interested should not be required to vote – bad decisions in the voting booth contribute to bad government."

[2 marks- evidence linked from Source 1 and 3]

Resources must be allocated to determine whether those who failed to vote have "valid and sufficient" reasons. Source 1 also says "millions of dollars are spent on checking up on those who didn't turn up." In the state of Queensland almost $1 million in state funds has been allocated to chase up those who failed to vote. This is a lot of money.

[3 marks – evidence linked from Source 1 and 3]

Reference to aspects of the following will be credited:
- It's unfair to punish people for not voting – only 37% of people think you should be fined (Source 1)
- Some people cannot get to polling stations due to genuine reasons ("poor people don't have a way to get to their voting place unlike rich people who have cars.") (Source 3)

Reasons for rejecting the other option:
Eileen Smith in Source 3 says "Forcing the population to vote means they will just deliberately spoil their ballot papers to avoid a fine" and in Source 2 it is clear that in all of the countries with compulsory voting, the number of informal ballot papers are much higher (eg Brazil it is 8.64% compared to only 0.7% in Canada). Source 1 shows that 9% of Australians have at some point registered an informal vote.
[3 marks – evaluative terminology, detailed evidence from Sources 1, 2 and 3]

Part F : World Issues

1. *Candidates can be credited in a number of ways **up to a maximum of 4 marks**.*

Possible approaches to answering the question:

Organisations send aid to help starving people. (1 mark)

The UN provide tents and medicines for refugees. (2 marks)

Charities such as the Red Cross provide experts such as doctors and nurses to areas where natural disasters have occurred, eg they spent many millions of pounds on field hospitals to help the victims of the typhoon in the Philippines. (3 marks)

Reference to aspects of the following will be credited: (Answers may vary greatly depending on the international conflict or issue studied.)
- Food/water/emergency relief
- Medical equipment/experts/medicines/vaccinations
- Peace talks/treaty negotiations
- Economic sanctions
- UN resolutions
- Economic Aid
- Specialist workers – engineers, scientists etc
- Financial Aid through the world bank
- UN may hold peace talks, eg with Syrian government during times of conflict. Pressure for government to resign

2. *Candidates can be credited in a number of ways **up to a maximum of 6 marks**.*

Possible approaches to answering the question:

HIV/Aids is caused by poor education. (1 mark)

Terrorism usually happens when a group of people feel they have been badly treated by a government. For example the Boston bombings were carried out by people who thought they had been unfairly treated by the USA. (2 marks)

Piracy is a major problem especially off the north east coast of Africa. Many poor people in Somalia are forced or persuaded to hi-jack ships and to take hostages by local gangs. There can be more money in it than there is in fishing. (3 marks)

Reference to aspects of the following will be credited:
- War in Afghanistan – response to terror/establish democracy
- The "Arab Spring" – demand for human rights, impact of internet
- International Debt – corruption, poverty, war, Western banks
- Poverty/Famine – natural disaster, war, climate, corruption, unfair trade
- Illegal immigration – poverty, famine, war

3. *Candidates can be credited in a number of ways up to a maximum of 10 marks.*

Possible approaches to answering the question:

OPTION 1

NATO should send troops to Country A as 140 000 people have been killed.
[1 mark – evidence from Source 1]

Source 1 points out that free elections were never held and that many people see democracy as the solution. Andy N from source three agrees that democracy is the solution.
[2 marks – evidence linked from Source 1 and Source 3]

It is believed that the President has used chemical weapons to kill 600 of his own people (S1). David W argues that we cannot stand by and watch this happen and a massive majority of 85% of those asked in Source 2 agree that NATO should do everything it can to stop chemical weapons.
[3 mark – evaluative terminology, evidence linked from Source 1, 2 and 3]

Reference to aspects of the following will be credited:
- The people want democratic reform (Sources 1 and/or 3)
- Many civilians have been killed (Sources 1 and/or 3).
- It worked in Libya, so why not in Country A? ie NATO got rid of Gaddafi (Source 3)
- People want chemical attacks stopped (Sources 2 and 3)
- NATO needs friendly Middle Eastern governments (Sources 1 and/or 2)

Reasons for rejecting the other option:
Source one tells us that the UK and the USA would like a friendlier government in Country A. 59% (a majority) of those asked in Source 2 agree that this is vital for NATO, so option 2 (doing nothing) is not a good option. (3 marks – evidence from two sources with an evaluative comment.)

OPTION 2

NATO should not send troops to Country A as 54% of the public strongly disagree.
[1 mark – evidence from Source 2]

NATO should not send troops to Country A as the majority of those questioned think that NATO cannot afford it. 27% agree and 42% strongly agree, this is well over half.
[2 marks – evidence from Source 2 with evaluative comment]

The vast majority, 83% think that sending NATO troops to Country A would not help the refugees (Source 2). Two million refugees really need help as they are living in terrible conditions (Source 3). So option two should not be followed.
[3 marks – evidence linked from Source 2 and 3 with evaluative comment]

Reference to aspects of the following will be credited:
- Cost is too high (Source 2 and Source 3)
- More troops make things worse (Source 1, Source 2 and Source 3)
- Wouldn't help refugees (Source 2 and Source 3)
- Loss of life would be too much (Source 3)

Reasons for rejecting the other option:
A huge majority of people in NATO countries (69%) believe that NATO cannot afford any more missions. (Source 2) This is supported by information from Source 3 which shows that the Libyan conflict cost the UK and USA alone, $21.5 billion without using ground troops.
(3 marks – evaluative terminology, detailed evidence from Sources 2 and 3)

NATIONAL 5 MODERN STUDIES 2015

Section 1

Part A: Democracy in Scotland

1. *Candidates can be credited in a number of ways up to a maximum of 4 marks.*

   Possible approaches to answering the question:

   Councils provide services such as education.
   [1 mark – accurate but undeveloped point]

   Councils provide services such as education. They provide education from 3-18 in schools.
   [2 marks – accurate with development]

   Dundee City is one of Scotland's 32 local councils. Education is a key service. Nurseries, primary and secondary schools are all funded by the Council. They employ the teachers and people such as janitors to provide the service.
   [3 marks – accurate point with development and detailed exemplification]

   Credit reference to aspects of the following:

   Some pupils may refer to the types of services and should be credited for this.

   Mandatory services – such as schooling for 5 – 16 year olds, social work services.

   Discretionary services – swimming pools, mobile libraries.

   Permissive powers such as economic development, recreation services; and,

   Regulatory powers – Local Authorities provide regulatory services such as trading standards and environmental health and issue licences for taxis and public houses.

   Councils deliver a wide range of valuable services to their local area. The main services they provide, in addition to their regulatory and licensing functions, are:
   - Education
   - Social Work
   - Roads and transport
   - Economic Development
   - Housing and the Built Environment
   - The Environment
   - Libraries
   - Waste management
   - Arts, Culture and Sport

   Councils also work with external agencies such as the police and fire service to provide community safety.

   Any other valid point that meets the criteria described in the general marking instructions for this kind of question (see column to left).

2. *Candidates can be credited in a number of ways up to a maximum of 6 marks.*

   Possible approaches to answering the question:

   People may choose to use the media to influence people.
   [1 mark – accurate but undeveloped point]

   People may join a trade union to protect their rights at work eg teachers join the EIS.
   [2 marks – accurate with development]

People may join a trade union to protect their rights at work eg teachers join the EIS. They might do this because they feel that they are not getting paid enough money and that the union will take action for them eg talking to their employers.

[3 marks – accurate point with development and exemplification]

People may choose to join a pressure group such as Greenpeace because they are worried about the environment and they feel they can't make any difference on their own. Joining a pressure group means lots of people campaign together so they have more of an impact eg Greenpeace have 11,000 Scottish members, this gives them strength in numbers and increases their collective influence on the government. This makes them difficult to ignore.

[4 marks – relevant accurate point with development, analysis and exemplification]

Credit reference to aspects of the following:

Pressure Groups
- Believe strongly about an issue such as human rights, the environment.
- Collective action more effective than individual.
- Media pay more attention to organised pressure groups.
- Pressure groups have experience of campaigning etc.
- Seen as the best way to influence government in between elections.

Trade Unions
- Protect rights at work eg health and safety, pay, holidays, pensions.
- TU have experience negotiating with management.
- TU have legal teams you can use.
- Collective action more effective than individual.

The Media
- Use them to get wider attention for an issue you care about eg newspapers are widely read.
- Legal way to get attention for your cause.
- Local and national appeal.
- Use of different media types eg Facebook campaigns.

3. *Candidates can be credited in a number of ways **up to a maximum of 10 marks**.*

Possible approaches to answering the question:

For Option 1:

I would choose Daisy as she has experience as a councillor.
[1 mark – evidence drawn from Source 1]

In Source 1 Daisy says that health needs to improve as lives are being cut short. She is right as life expectancy is less in Glenlochy.
[2 marks – evaluative terminology with limited evidence from Source 1 and Source 2]

In Source 1 Daisy states that "The lives of people in Glenlochy are being cruelly cut short". She is correct as Source 2 states life expectancy is only 77 years compared to 79 in the rest of Scotland, a significant difference of two years.
[3 marks – evidence drawn from two Sources with detailed use of evidence and evaluative terminology]

Reference to aspects of the following will be credited:
- Local Councillor [Source 1] – constituents want an experienced politician [Source 2].
- Source 1 – "I will work to ensure that more women are elected" Source 2 – 54% agree.
- 54% think the Scottish parliament needs more female MSPs [Source 2] and Daisy as a female would be a good choice [Source 1].

- Source 1 – number of women working locally – Source 3 – only 34% in Glenlochy but 45% in Scotland.
- Source 1 – unemployment a problem – true as 9% unemployed in Glenlochy and 7% in Scotland [Source 3].
- Childcare is a problem [Source 1] – 68% in Source 2 agree.

Against Option 1

Daisy claims a lack of internet access is an obvious barrier however Source 3 shows 3% more households in Glenlochy have access to the internet [2 marks].

Reference to aspects of the following will be credited:
- A lack of internet access [Source 1] – but Source 3 shows 79% have access compared to 76% in Scotland.
- Crime is not a concern [Source 1] but Source 2 shows 530 people attended a local meeting and raised valid concerns.
- Crime is not a concern [Source 1] Source 2 – 65% disagree with her.
- Daisy says health needs to improve but there are fewer long term illnesses in Glenlochy, 3% less than the UK [Source 3].
- Community council say a legal background is necessary [Source 2] but Daisy doesn't have this [Source 1].

For Option 2:

I would choose Tom because he has experience as a lawyer and Source 2 says our new MSPs should have a legal background.
[2 marks – evidence drawn from Sources 1 and 2]

Tom says that employment is a key issue which has to be improved [Source1]. He is right as Source 3 shows that unemployment is higher in Glenlochy.
[2 marks – evidence drawn from Sources 1 and 3]

In Source 1 – Tom says that "Too few people are in full time work. He is right as Glenlochy's full time employment rate is 6% lower than the rest of Scotland according to Source 3. This is clearly a problem, especially as according to Source 2 there is only one major employer in the local area and it recently made 100 people redundant.
[3 marks – evidence drawn from 3 Sources with detailed use of evidence and evaluative terminology]

Reference to aspects of the following will be credited:
- Source 1 – Tom is a lawyer and Source 2 – local people worried about crime would like an MSP with a legal background.
- Source 1 – too few people are in full time work and Source 3 shows only 42% working compared to 48%.
- Source 1 – many relying on benefits and Source 3 shows 1.7% more claimants in Glenlochy compared to Scotland as whole.
- Source 1 – crime is a major concern and Source 2 shows 530 people attended a meeting to voice concerns.
- Source 1 – crime is a major concern and Source 2 shows 65% of people agree it's a problem.

Against Option 2

Tom claims that a lack of childcare isn't a problem in Glenlochy but 68% of local people think it is a major problem [2 marks].

Reference to aspects of the following will be credited:
- "The majority of local people agree with me that elderly people are well cared for" [Source 1] but Source 2 shows only 35% agree.
- Childcare not a problem [Source 1] – Source 2 68% feel it is.

- Tom says too many are leaving school before S6 [Source 1] – this isn't the case according to Source 3 – 2% more stay to S6 than the Scottish average.
- Many feel Glenlochy needs an experience representative [Source 2] and Tom has no experience as a representative [Source 1].

Part B: Democracy in the United Kingdom

4. *Candidates can be credited in a number of ways* **up to a maximum of 4 marks.**

Possible approaches to answering the question:

They examine government decisions.
[1 mark – accurate but undeveloped point]

The Lords can delay government bills by a year if they disagree.
[2 marks – accurate with development]

The Lords can contribute to government decision making as some of them can hold positions in the Cabinet and attend Cabinet meetings eg Baroness Stowell. Members of the House of Lords have been appointed to other government posts in recent years.
[3 marks – accurate point with development and exemplification]

Credit reference to aspects of the following:
- Provides detailed scrutiny and discussion of legislation due to experience and expertise of members.
- Can amend or reject legislation (limited by Parliament Acts).
- Can introduce bills (not money bills).
- May be able to force government to rethink legislation or policy as opposition in the Lords is often bad publicity for the government.
- Peers can be appointed as government ministers and some do attend full cabinet meetings.

5. *Candidates can be credited in a number of ways* **up to a maximum of 6 marks.**

Possible approaches to answering the question:

People may choose to use the media to influence people.
[1 mark – accurate but undeveloped point]

People may join a trade union to protect their rights at work eg rail workers join the Rail, Maritime and Transport Union (RMT).
[2 marks – accurate with development]

People may join a trade union to protect their rights at work eg rail workers join the Rail, Maritime and Transport Union (RMT). They might do this because they feel that they are not getting paid enough money and that the union will take action for them eg talking to their employers.
[3 marks – accurate point with development and exemplification]

People may choose to join a pressure group such as Greenpeace because they are worried about the environment and they feel they can't make any difference on their own. Joining a pressure group means lots of people campaign together so they have more of an impact eg Greenpeace have 130,000 UK supporters, this gives them strength in numbers and increases their collective influence on the government. This makes them difficult to ignore.
[4 marks – relevant accurate point with development, analysis and exemplification]

Credit reference to aspects of the following:

Pressure Groups
- Believe strongly about an issue such as human rights, the environment.
- Collective action more effective than individual.
- Media pay more attention to organised pressure groups.
- Pressure groups have experience of campaigning etc.
- Seen as the best way to influence government in between elections.

Trades Unions
- Protect rights at work eg health and safety, pay, holidays, pensions.
- TU have experience negotiating with management.
- TU have legal teams you can use.
- Collective action more effective than individual.

The Media
- Use them to get wider attention for an issue you care about eg newspapers are widely read.
- Legal way to get attention for your cause.
- Local and national appeal.
- Use of different media types eg Facebook campaigns.

6. *Candidates can be credited in a number of ways* **up to a maximum of 10 marks.**

Possible approaches to answering the question:

OPTION 1

For Option 1:

I would choose Nora as she has experience as a councillor.
[1 mark – evidence drawn from Source 1]

In Source 1 Nora says that health needs to improve as lives are being cut short. She is right as life expectancy is less in Millwood.
[2 marks – evaluative terminology with limited evidence from Source 1 and Source 2]

In Source 1 Nora states that "The lives of people in Millwood are being cruelly cut short". She is correct as Source 2 states life expectancy is only 77 years compared to 80 in the rest of the UK, a significant difference of three years.
[3 marks – evidence drawn from 2 Sources with detailed use of evidence and evaluative terminology]

Reference to aspects of the following will be credited:
- Local Councillor [Source 1] – constituents want an experienced politician [Source 2].
- Source 1 – more women are elected – Source 2 54% agree.
- Source 1 – number of women working locally – Source 3 only 34% in Millwood but 45% in UK.
- Source 1 – unemployment a problem; true as 9% unemployed in Millwood and 6% in UK [Source 3].
- Childcare is a problem [Source 1] and 68% in Source 2 agree.

Against Option 1

Nora claims a lack of internet access is an obvious barrier however Source 3 shows 2% more households in Millwood have access to the internet [2 marks].

Reference to aspects of the following will be credited:
- Source 1 – a lack of internet access Source 1 – but Source 3 shows 79% have access compared to 77% in UK.
- Source 1 – crime is not a problem but Source 2 shows 530 people attended a local meeting and raised valid concerns.
- Source 1 – crime is not a problem – Source 2 – 61% disagree with Nora.

- Nora says health needs to improve but there are fewer long term illnesses in Millwood, 3% less than the UK [Source 3].
- Community council say a legal background [Source 2] is necessary but Nora doesn't have this [Source 1].

For Option 2:

I would choose John because he is a lawyer and Source 2 says our new MP should have a legal background.
[2 marks – evidence drawn from Sources 1 and 2]

John says that employment is a key issue which has to be improved (Source1). He is right as Source 3 shows 9% of Millwood are unemployed compared to 6% of UK.
[2 marks – evidence drawn from Sources 1 and 3]

In Source 1 John says that "Too few people are in full time work. He is right as Millwood's full time employment rate is 7% lower than the UK's.

This is clearly a problem, especially as according to Source 2 there is only one major employer in the local area and it recently made 100 people redundant.
[3 marks – evidence drawn from 3 Sources with detailed use of evidence and evaluative terminology]

Reference to aspects of the following will be credited:
- Source 1 – John is a lawyer and Source 2 shows local people are worried about crime and would like an MP with a legal background.
- Source 1 – too few people are in full time work and Source 3 shows only 42% working compared to 49%.
- Source 1 – too many relying on benefits – Source 3 shows 2.3% more claimants in Millwood.
- Source 1 – crime is a major concern and Source 2 shows 530 people attended a meeting to voice concerns.
- Source 1 – crime is a major concern and 61% of people agree it's a problem [Source 2].

Against Option 2

John claims that a lack of childcare isn't a problem in Millwood but 68% of local people think it is a major problem [2 marks].

Reference to aspects of the following will be credited:
- The majority agree elderly are well cared for but Source 2 shows only 35% agree.
- Childcare not a problem – Source 2 68% feel it is.
- John says too many are leaving school before S6 – this isn't the case according to Source 3 – 3% more stay to S6 than the UK average.

Section 2

Part C: Social Inequality

7. *Candidates can be credited in a number of ways up to a maximum of 4 marks.*

Possible approaches to answering the question:

The Government has tried to reduce social inequalities by encouraging people to make better lifestyle choices.
[1 mark – accurate but undeveloped point]

The Government has tried to reduce social inequalities in housing by providing Social Housing to those who need it, to make sure everyone has an acceptable standard of housing.
[2 marks – accurate with development]

The Government has tried to reduce social inequalities in education by providing free state education. They also reduce inequalities within education by providing free school meals and clothing vouchers to pupils from lower income backgrounds.
[3 marks – accurate point with development and exemplification]

Credit reference to aspects of the following:
- **Health:** Passing Laws, providing free health care, issuing public guidelines (smoking/exercise/healthy eating).
- **Education:** Educational Maintenance Allowance (EMA); Student Loans; Scholarships and bursaries.
- **Housing:** Housing benefit.
- **Discrimination:** Equality Act 2010, Equality & Human Rights Commission (EHRC).
- **Welfare Benefits:** the government provides a huge range of benefits for the elderly, families, out of work, disabled etc.

8. Candidates can be credited in a number of ways up to a maximum of 8 marks.

Possible approaches to answering the question:

Ethnic minorities still face inequality in society because they still face racism in some areas of society.
[1 mark – accurate but undeveloped point]

Older people still face inequality in society because they face discrimination in the world of work because some employers think they don't have IT skills.
[2 marks – accurate with development]

Women still face inequality in society because of sexism. Employers, for example, might not want to employ a woman as they think she will need time off to look after her children. This means that women find it more difficult to find suitable work and as a result often work part-time in occupations like cleaning, childcare etc. Many women feel that the glass ceiling still exists which limits opportunities for promotion in their careers.
[4 marks – accurate point with development, analysis and exemplification]

Credit reference to aspects of the following:
- **Ethnic Minorities:** Prejudice, language barriers, poor educational attainment, higher unemployment rates, specific health issues.
- **Older People:** Ageism; financial preparation for retirement; previous occupation; family support; changes to benefit system, ie bedroom tax and employability.
- **Women:** Sexism; glass ceiling; pay gap; employment in 5C's, childcare availability and costs.
- **Disabled:** Prejudice; over qualification; lack of work experience; family support network; continuing health issues; reliance on benefits.
- **Lone Parents:** Prejudice, family commitments, lack of qualifications, no support network/childcare.
- **Unemployed:** Stigma of long term unemployment, lack of experience,
- Changes to the benefit system, the recession.

9. *Candidates can be credited in a number of ways up to a maximum of 8 marks.*

Possible approaches to answering the question:

The impact of poverty on a child's life

Conclusion – Poverty can have a big impact on a child's health.
[1 mark – valid conclusion]

Poverty can have a big impact on a child's health. [Mark 1 – valid conclusion] For example, life expectancy for the poorest children is only 71 years [Source 2].

[2 marks – conclusion and evidence from one source]

Conclusion – Poverty can have a big impact on many areas of a child's life [1 mark valid conclusion]. Children living in poverty find themselves socially excluded from everyday life [Source 1]. Sixty two percent of poor families cannot afford a week's holiday compared to only 6% of wealthy families [Source 2].

[3 marks – conclusion and information from two sources]

Conclusion – Poverty can have a big impact on many areas of a child's health. [1 mark valid conclusion] This is backed up by figures which show life expectancy at birth is 71 years for poor children, compared to 82 years for wealthy children [Source 2]. This is a substantial difference of eleven years.

[3 marks – conclusion and information from two sources with evaluative terminology]

The Government's progress towards meeting its targets for 2020.

Conclusion – The Government will make little progress in the next few years.

[1 mark – valid conclusion]

Conclusion – The Government has made little progress toward reducing child poverty in the UK [1 mark valid conclusion]. Source 2 shows us that both relative and absolute poverty will continue to increase.

[2 marks – conclusion and evidence from one source]

Conclusion – The Government will make little progress toward reducing child poverty in the UK [1 mark valid conclusion]. Currently, a quarter of children live in poverty in the UK [Source 1]. Government made a promise to reduce child poverty to 12% for relative poverty by 2020 [Source 1] but Source 3 shows it will actually be 22%.

[3 marks – conclusion and information from two sources]

UK Poverty rates compared to other Countries

Conclusion – UK child poverty rates are higher than most other EU countries

[1 mark valid conclusion]

Conclusion – UK child poverty rates are higher than most other EU countries

[1 mark valid conclusion]

Currently a quarter of children are living in poverty in the UK [Source 1], this is 4% higher than the EU average of 21% [Source 3].

[3 marks – conclusion and evidence from two sources]

Conclusion – UK child poverty rates are among the highest in the EU [1 mark valid conclusion]. Only three EU countries have higher rates of child poverty than the UK, these are Romania, Spain and Italy which are all above the UKs rate of 25% [Source 3]. The UK is also above the EU average of 21% [Source 3].

[3 marks – conclusion and evidence from two sources]

Part D: Crime and the Law

10. *Candidates can be credited in a number of ways **up to a maximum of 4 marks.***

They can send people to prison.

[1 mark – accurate but undeveloped point]

They can convict criminals and send them to prison. The Sheriff Court can sentence someone for up to five years.

[2 marks – accurate point with development]

They can convict criminals and send them to prison. The Sheriff Court can sentence someone for up to five years. However, if the Sheriff feels this is an insufficient penalty they can refer the case to the High Court where a life sentence is possible.

[3 marks – accurate point with development and exemplification]

Credit reference to aspects of the following:
- Fines
- Community Service
- Community Payback Orders
- Curfews
- ASBOs
- Electronic Tagging

11. *Candidates can be credited in a number of ways **up to a maximum of 8 marks.***

Possible approaches to answering the question:

Drug addiction can cause crime.

[1 mark – accurate but undeveloped point]

Drug addiction can cause crime as addicts need to pay for their drugs and need to steal to fund their habit.

[2 marks – accurate point with development]

Drug addiction can cause crime as addicts need to pay for their drugs and need to steal to fund their habit. Those with drug use dependency are more likely to be arrested for crimes such as burglary, shoplifting or for robbery and handling stolen goods.

[3 marks – accurate point with development and exemplification]

Credit reference to aspects of the following:
- Poverty/deprivation
- Peer pressure
- Family influence
- Alcohol abuse
- Mental Illness
- Violent media images
- Homelessness
- Poor Educational Attainment
- Social Exclusion
- Greed – White collar crime

12. Candidates can be credited in a number of ways up to a maximum of 8 marks.

The level of public awareness of the law concerning social media

Conclusion – A minority of people know about the law.

[1 mark – valid conclusion]

Conclusion – A minority of people know about the law [1 mark – valid conclusion]. This is supported by Source 1 which shows only 1 in 10 know about the law.

[2 marks – conclusion and evidence from one source]

Conclusion – A minority of people know about the law
[1 mark – valid conclusion]. This is supported by Source
1 which shows only 1 in 10 know about the law and by
Source 2 which tells us 75% of people, a clear majority
didn't know about the consequences of being offensive.
[3 marks – conclusion and information from two
sources with evaluative terminology]

- More than half of sixteen to eighteen year olds
believed it was illegal for an employer to check social
media [Source 1].

Social media and the workplace

Conclusion – Employees now have more. rules to follow
about the use of social media.
[1 mark – valid conclusion]

Conclusion – Employees now have more rules to
follow about the use of social media. [1 mark – valid
conclusion] The Gleninch Council have issued a memo
to its employees on the appropriate use of social media
during work-time [Source 2].
[2 marks – conclusion and evidence from one source]

Conclusion – A lot of working time is being lost due to
the use of social media. [1 mark – valid conclusion]
The Gleninch Council have issued a memo to its
employees on the appropriate use of social media during
work-time [Source 2]. This is obviously a problem judging
by the increase in the number of hours lost through
social media breaks from half an hour to two hours per
day [Source 3].
[3 marks – conclusion and information from two sources]
- Social Media breaks are costing more than smoking
breaks [Source 3].
- Social Media breaks have quadrupled since 2010
[Source 2].
- Companies now use Social Media to vet applicants
[Source 1].
- The Gleninch Council may sack people for
inappropriate use of Social Media [Source 2].

Crime associated with social media

Conclusion – There has been an increase in prosecutions
relating to social media.
[1 mark – valid conclusion]

Conclusion – There has been an increase in prosecutions
relating to social media [1 mark – valid conclusion].
Source 3 shows a huge increase in successful prosecutions.
[2 marks – conclusion and evidence from one source]

Conclusion – Crime related to social media appears
to have increased in recent years [1 mark – valid
conclusion]. Source 2 shows an increase in the number
of incidents reported to the police from 2347 to 2703.
However, police have said that many of these (two
thirds) are petty online arguments [Source 1].
[3 marks – conclusion and information from two sources]

- More and more people are being prosecuted for their
online activities [Source 1].
- Both the number of complaints to the police and of
successful prosecutions have increased [Source 2].

Section 3

Part E: World Powers

13. Candidates can be credited in a number of ways up to a
maximum of 6 marks.

Possible approaches to answering the question:

CHINA
Other countries rely on China for trade.
[1 mark – accurate but undeveloped point]

North Korea relies on China for both military aid and for
food supplies to feed its population.
[2 marks – accurate point with exemplification]

China now manufactures more goods than any other
country in the world eg 70% of the world's toys and 50%
of the world's clothes. Consumers in places like the USA
and the EU rely on China for cheap goods.
[3 marks – accurate point with development and
exemplification]

RUSSIA
Other countries rely on Russia for gas supply.
[1 mark – accurate but undeveloped point]

Russia has political influence in the UN. This is because it
has a permanent place in the UNSC.
[2 marks – accurate point with exemplification]

The government of Ukraine wanted to build closer
economic ties with Western Europe. The recent unrest
in Ukraine was a result of conflict between some of
their people, who want to stay close to Russia, and their
government. Russia has used its military power to arm
some Ukrainians which has encouraged a civil war in the
eastern parts of the country.
[3 marks – accurate point with development and
exemplification]

USA
Other countries rely on the USA for military support.
[1 mark – accurate but undeveloped point]

The US Dollar is like an international currency. Oil is sold
in dollars per barrel.
[2 marks – accurate point with exemplification]

The United States has a 'special relationship' with the
United Kingdom, a phrase used to describe the close
political and economic relations between both countries.
Britain has been the USA's strongest supporter in the War
on Terror eg bombing IS in Iraq and Syria.
[3 marks – accurate point with development and
exemplification]

Credit reference to aspects of the following:
- Trade
- Culture
- Defence
- Diplomatic support
- Ideology
- Environment
- Economic migration
- Finance/Banking
- International Organisations

14. Candidates can be credited in a number of ways **up to a
maximum of 6 marks.**

Possible approaches to answering the question:

CHINA
Some people are poorly represented in government as
they are not in the Communist Party.
[1 mark – accurate point with no development]

Those living and working in rural areas are poorly
represented in national government as they are less
likely to be members of the Communist Party. The rural
Chinese can take part in local committees but these

tend to only focus on local issues and not on provincial, national or international issues.

[3 marks – accurate point with development and exemplification]

Credit reference to the following:
- Income/poverty
- Urban/rural divide
- Gender – national government still dominated by men
- Party membership is limited and has restrictions
- Migrant workers may not be registered and cannot participate
- Those with anti-communist views or those who support democratic reform are not well represented and are often silenced by the authorities
- Pressure group activists are not represented especially if they oppose the Communist system

USA
Black Americans are not well represented as there are few Black role models in government.

[1 mark – accurate but undeveloped point]

Black Americans are not well represented as they are more likely to be poor. This tends to mean that they are less likely to run for office.

[2 marks – accurate point with development]

Hispanic Americans are less likely to be represented in government as there is a much lower participation rate among Hispanics. Some have difficulty as English is not their first language so politics and government is difficult for them to understand. This leads to fewer Latinos being elected to high office such as Governor or Senator.

[3 marks – accurate point with development and exemplification]

Credit reference to the following:
- Low paid unskilled work/white collar jobs. Difference in participation leads to difference in representation.
- Blacks and Hispanics experience social and economic inequality as a result of poverty. Apathetic, no role models, other priorities.
- Women remain underrepresented as they either do not run for office or are not chosen by the big two parties, despite the fact that women are more likely to vote in presidential elections.
- Poorly educated are poorly represented and are less likely to vote.
- Some recent immigrants may not have legal status and may lack representation as a result.
- Homeless people may be unlikely to vote and lack representation.

15. *Candidates can be credited in a number of ways* **up to a maximum of 8 marks.**

Possible approaches to answering the question:

Evidence to support the view of Kirsten Nunez

In the USA levels of crime have fallen sharply.

[1 mark – accurate use of Source 1 but minimal development]

In the USA levels of crime have fallen sharply. A study from Harvard University says there is no evidence which proves widespread gun ownership among the general population leads to higher incidents of murder.

[2 marks – accurate use of information from different parts of Source 1]

In the USA levels of crime have fallen sharply. A study from Harvard University says there is no evidence which proves widespread gun ownership among the

general population leads to higher incidents of murder. This is backed by Source 2 which shows that France has comparatively few gun deaths and they allow gun ownership.

[3 marks – accurate use of information from Sources 1 and 2]

Credit reference to aspects of the following:
- France allows gun ownership but has the second lowest murder rate [Source 3].
- France allows gun ownership but has approximately one third of the violent crime that Russia has [Source 3].
- USA has the highest gun ownership rate but has less than half the murder rate that Russia has [Source 3].

Evidence to oppose the view of Kirsten Nunez

In Source 1 The Brady Campaign to Prevent Gun Violence found that the U.S. firearm homicide rate is 20 times higher than the combined rates of 22 countries with similar levels of wealth.

[1 mark – accurate use of Source 1 but minimal development]

Kristen is wrong as Japan is clearly the safest country as it has by far the lowest murder rate and it does not allow guns of any kind.

[2 marks – accurate use of information from two different Sources]

Credit reference to aspects of the following:
- USA allows gun ownership but has the highest rates of robbery [Source 3].
- Brazil allows guns but has the second highest rate of violent crime and the highest murder rate [Source 3]. Also from Source 2 it has the highest gun deaths.

Part F: World Issues

16. *Candidates can be credited in a number of ways* **up to a maximum of 6 marks.**

African people living in poverty often go hungry.

[1 mark – accurate but undeveloped point]

During a conflict many people have become refugees as their homes have been destroyed by armed forces.

[2 marks – accurate point with development]

Many children in countries like Botswana have been left orphaned by AIDS. This has denied them an education and resulted in a lifetime of poverty. Their health will also be affected as they will be unable to afford health care.

[3 marks – accurate point with development and exemplification]

Credit reference to aspects of the following:
- Poverty
- Ill-health
- Crime/violent assault/murder/rape
- Child soldiers/child labour/child abduction
- Loss of family
- Homeless
- Terrorism
- Piracy
- Nuclear Weapons
- Refugees
- Loss of liberty/kidnapping
- Loss of property/business/job

No marks should be awarded for the identification of the world issue or problem.

17. *Candidates can be credited in a number of ways **up to a maximum of 8 marks**.*

Possible approaches to answering the question:

The conflict in Ukraine has not been solved by the EU as Russia is providing arms to the rebels.
[1 mark – accurate but undeveloped point]

The UN has tried to stop the recent Israel/Palestine conflict by arranging peace talks. It failed as Israel was determined to stop rockets being fired at its territory and ignored the invitation to the peace talks.
[2 marks – accurate point with development]

Piracy is a big problem off the coast of Somalia. The NATO naval task force has been successful as it has around 25 warships which patrol the area and protect shipping. NATO ships have reduced the problem but the area involved is so large and the Somali's are so poor it is probably impossible to stop it totally.
[4 marks – accurate point with development, exemplification and analysis]

Credit reference to aspects of the following
- Libya – success as NATO military power was too much for Libya.
- Libya – failure as tribal/religious rivalries making progress difficult.
- Syria – failure of the UN to agree collective action – Russian veto.
- Syria – the UN have been successful in feeding refugees as they are in neighbouring countries which have offered assistance and are easier to reach.
- Terrorism – success as vast resources committed by NATO.
- Terrorism – failure – religious/ethnic/political feelings are too strong and cannot be easily controlled. Extremists are willing to give their own lives, which is difficult to combat.
- Child Soldiers – War Child has been successful in the Democratic Republic of Congo in that they have accommodated, rehabilitated and reintegrated children who have been displaced from their homes due to conflict.
- Child Soldiers – failure – much of the DR Congo is still desperately poor and still in conflict.

No marks should be awarded for the identification of the world issue or conflict.

18. Candidates can be credited in a number of ways up to a maximum of 8 marks.

Possible approaches to answering the question:

Evidence to support the view of Ted King

Two aid workers were shot dead in Afghanistan.
[1 mark – accurate source of Source 1 but minimal development]

Afghanistan is a drug producer and it is more dangerous because two aid workers were shot dead in Afghanistan while the murder rate in the USA (a drug using country) has halved.
[2 marks – accurate use of information from different parts of Source 1]

Afghanistan is a drug producer and it is more dangerous because two aid workers were shot dead. Afghanistan also has the second highest number of violent kidnappings. This figure is three times higher than for the highest drug using country, the USA.
[3 marks – accurate use of information from Sources 1 and 3 with evaluative comment]

Credit reference to aspects of the following:
- Colombia has "no-go" areas (Source 1).
- Colombia has highest murder rate (Source 3).
- Colombia has highest kidnapping rate (Source 3).
- All three producers have very high kidnappings (Source 3).
- El Salvador (user) has reduced its murder rate by 80% (Source 1).
- USA (user) murder rate has fallen (Source 1).

Evidence to oppose the view of Ted King

The USA is more dangerous as it has the most drug related crime at 104 per 100,000. This is nearly double the highest drug producing country, Colombia.
[2 marks – accurate use of Source 2 with evaluative comment]

Ted is wrong as the USA is more dangerous. One gang member admitted killing forty people and it has far more serious assaults at 874.
[2 marks – accurate use of information from two different Sources]

Ted is clearly wrong as the USA (not a drug producer) is more dangerous. One gang member admitted killing forty people and it has far more serious assaults than any of the drug producers at 874. The highest figure in the drug producing countries is 100 in Peru which is only around a ninth of the USA figure.
[3 marks – accurate use of information from two sources with evaluative comment]

Credit reference to aspects of the following:
- President says Afghanistan is safer (Source 1).
- Lowest total crime rates are in Colombia and Peru (Source 2).
- USA has highest total crime rate (Source 2).
- USA has most drug crime (Source 2).
- Afghanistan has the lowest murder rate (Source 3).
- USA has the most serious assaults (Source 3).

Acknowledgements

Permission has been sought from all relevant copyright holders and Hodder Gibson is grateful for the use of the following:

Figures from the table 'Who do you think performed best overall in the party leaders' debates?' taken from www.yougov.co.uk, public domain (Model Paper 1 page 7);
The logo for G8 Canada. Reproduced with permission of the Department of Foreign Affairs, Trade and Development Canada, Ottawa (Model Paper 1 page 19);
An extract from *The Dundee Courier* about the bridge tolls campaign © D.C. Thomson & Co. Ltd Dundee Scotland (Model Paper 3 page 4);
Image © Point Fr/Shutterstock.com (2015 page 4);
Image © Goodluz/Shutterstock.com (2015 page 4);
Image © Blend Images/Shutterstock.com (2015 page 8);
Image © Dean Drobot/Shutterstock.com (2015 page 8);
Image © Mahesh Patil/Shutterstock.com (2015 pages 20 & 24).

Hodder Gibson would like to thank SQA for use of any past exam questions that may have been used in model papers, whether amended or in original form.